BOGUS
BALANCE

To Shannon—
Here's to
your
Blissful life!

Copyright © 2015 Deirdre Maloney

Bogus Balance: Your Journey to *Real* Work/Life Bliss

ISBN: 978-0-9840273-5-4 paperback
           978-0-9840273-6-1 ebook

Cover and interior design by *the*BookDesigners, www.bookdesigners.com
Copyediting by Lisa Wolff

Printed in the United States of America

No part of this book may be reproduced, stored in a retrieval system,
transmitted in any form or by any means, electronic, mechanical, audio
recording or otherwise, without prior permission of the author and
publisher. Please direct comments and inquiries to:

Published by:

Business
Solutions
Press▬

113 West G Street, #647
San Diego, CA 92101
(619) 209-7749
www.makemomentum.com

Publisher's Cataloging in Publication Data

Maloney, Deirdre

    Bogus balance: your journey to real work/life bliss / Deirdre Maloney.
    –San Diego, CA: Business Solutions Press, c2015.

    p.;cm

    ISBN: 978-0-9840273-5-4 (pbk.) ; 978-0-9840273-6-1 (ebk)

    1. Self-help--Stress 2. Work/life balance 3. Business pressure 4.
    Balancing career and family   I. Title.

BOGUS BALANCE

YOUR JOURNEY TO *REAL* WORK/LIFE BLISS

DEIRDRE MALONEY

Business
Solutions
Press

San Diego, California

This book is dedicated to my blissfuls,
who have shined a big, bright light on my own path to bliss…
…and to Hubbie, for holding my hand every step of the way

CONTENTS

"I believe that the very purpose of life is to be happy."

—DALAI LAMA

PROLOGUE

I AM WRITING a book on balance. And I am in the midst of chaos.

No, really, I'm in the midst of chaos. Right now.

You see, in exactly 11 days I'm moving overseas. I'll be starting in Paris, then moving on to Barcelona. The trip will last six months, enough time to write this book.

That's the plan, anyway.

This trip means that for six months my business is pretty much on hold. It means that my lease is expiring and I have no backup plan, no "just in case." It means my husband (herein referred to as "Hubbie") does not have a job to return to, since he quit his longtime position so we could go on this trip. It means six months of adventure and returning to a whole lot of...TBD.

It's a pretty exciting (if not terrifying) turn of events. And I've got the perfect reason for doing it. Actually, I've got two reasons.

First, I'm writing this book. And what better place to write a book than where Hemingway himself put down a word or two...even if the idea of writing a book in Paris is more than a little clichéd?

Second, I myself have learned a few things by talking to blissful people as I prepared to write this book. By moving out of my comfort zone, by living in a new space and getting some perspective, I'm essentially putting into practice some of the lessons they so generously shared with me. Lessons you will soon learn as well.

You might be wondering why I'm telling you all of this. After all, this book is about *you* and *your* journey to bliss. It's about helping you create your own journey to your own blissful place, and finding true balance through it all. It's not about me.

Yet I thought it would interest you to know that, while writing this book, I'm on a journey, too. And that it's got me feeling pretty vulnerable. Which, as you'll soon learn, is perfectly okay. In fact, vulnerability is what many of us need to feel in order to get to bliss. And that's the ultimate goal.

Now, how this move overseas will actually go, how the experience will play out, and how my own blissful journey may be impacted remains to be seen.

So stay tuned. The epilogue will spill the beans about what went right, and what went…less than perfectly. I'm curious to see how things turn out myself.

In the meantime, enjoy the book.

I'll see you on the other side.

INTRODUCTION

The Why. The How.
The How to Use This Book.

WELCOME!

If you've cracked open this book, chances are you're not feeling very balanced. Or perhaps you're somewhat balanced but you're not blissful. Perhaps you're nowhere near it. Whatever the case, you're in the right place. It's great to have you!

If any of the above assumptions are true, know that you're not alone. Many people are in the same proverbial boat. Me included. So take a moment and relax, knowing we're all in this balance thing together.

And while you're relaxing, let's get a few things out of the way.

Though this book is filled with ideas and solutions to overcome the bogus balance phenomenon and find your bliss, most of them aren't mine. In fact, one of the things that excites me so much about this book is that I get to share the wisdom and advice of others who have figured this balance thing out. Actually, they've achieved more than balance. They've achieved true happiness. They're blissful. Bliss–*full*. Not just some of the time but most of it. And, let's be real, that's the goal.

After all, who really cares if we're balanced if it doesn't make us happy?

When I asked these people (whom I refer to as my blissfuls)

to describe their blissful lives, a few words continually popped up. *Happiness, joy* and *personal fulfillment* often made the cut. *Peaceful* and *tranquil* were also a big part of their blissful lives. Many mentioned that feeling like they gave back in some way was critically important to their bliss. Some said their bliss was about a series of interspersed, joyful moments in their lives, while others identified a more constant feeling. Whatever the case, the bliss was an underlying presence, a regular part of their lives. One they always returned to. In fact, they wouldn't stand for anything else.

We'll get back to these wise folks, what bliss means to them and how they've achieved it, in a moment.

First…a bit of background.

WHY I WROTE THIS BOOK

I'll admit it. Over my lifetime I have explored various ideas and tips about balancing work and life, about finding happiness by having it all, every day. I believed it all wholeheartedly. It didn't even sound that hard. And yet, when I tried to do it, when I tried to balance my life and feel sane, I fell flat on my face. And, when I asked around, I found out that many, many others had done the same. A bunch of us just felt like we were drowning throughout the day…beginning from the moment we woke up.

I wrote this book because, in the end, I decided that we all deserved to hear the truth. Which is that balance in the way so many of us have learned about it is just unattainable. That it's completely bogus.

It's a big problem, this false idea that work/life balance is something we can achieve if we just try hard enough.

We're surrounded by these bogus messages all the time. They tell us that if we just put our minds to it, if we adopt 10 tips and the perfect scheduling tool we can have it all—the most successful career, the most fulfilling life, permanent happiness—no sweat. Articles and books and blog posts are all written about having it all. All around us are interviews with smiling people who talk about how they've managed to juggle their career and parenthood, all while keeping their marriage healthy and their squeaky-clean children behaving perfectly.

I believed it all. I actually first learned these bogus lessons as a little girl, when I began hearing a whole lot of women talking about how they—and any of us—could have it all.

- They talked about professional careers and a family—all managed perfectly. Because times were changing.

- They talked about moving up at the office and cuddling close with their husbands. All with warm, sophisticated grace.

- They discussed their circles of support, told stories of how they impressed their bosses with their brilliance, spun tales of how—through it all—they still had time to attend their kids' pageants and cook the best-ever chicken stock from scratch.

Now, before going any further, *please* hear me when I say that despite the examples above, this book is not for women only. I know plenty of men who are dealing with this whole bogus balance issue. I just happened to be brought up around messages about the perfect feminist revolution, the one that paved the way for people like me to have all kinds of opportunities… opportunities that I simply *couldn't* let fall away, for that would be a waste. And a shame. It wasn't just an opportunity to have it all, but my duty to do so.

And so I tried hard to have it all, and I struggled continually.

I'd get some momentum going on the work front, but I found my friendships would begin to slip. I'd take some time to see my family, but I'd fail to meet a writing deadline. I began traveling more as I booked more speaking engagements, but Hubbie and I became distant. All throughout this time I became less and less healthy, the circles under my eyes growing darker, the tension in my face growing stronger, the belly laughs nonexistent, and the anxiety of trying to be awesome at everything eating away at any of the happiness I did achieve.

And I felt like a failure. Silently I'd struggle with what felt like a complete weakness on my part to hold things together, berating myself for feeling so chaotic and tired and…not happy… so frequently. I told myself to get it together.

I told myself I needed to find my balance once and for all. I told myself to ask around, since others seemed to have it all figured out. I decided that would help me get there.

So I looked into it. I did indeed ask around. A lot. And that's when I realized the truth.

Everyone else was struggling, too. They struggled silently, it seemed, hurrying from one place and task to the next, barely taking time to breathe (never mind smile). It turned out that despite all of the books and the seminars, everyone around me was struggling to have it all, and they couldn't achieve it either.

It turned out that work/life balance wasn't as simple as 10 steps. In fact, the more I thought about it and the more I suffered from trying to achieve it, the more I realized that work/life balance is unattainable—perhaps impossible—for most of us. At least, it's impossible in the way society likes to define it.

And yet few of us have realized it. Or if we've realized it, we haven't embraced it. Instead we strive for the perfect balance, the perfect solution, the perfect life in every way…and we completely set ourselves up for lots of stress accompanied by a sense of failure. We attend seminars and chat deeply with each other and create strategies to keep it all together perfectly, to achieve everything our society tells us we can—and should—achieve. We struggle to move up at work while keeping our kids thriving and our marriages passionately fulfilled. Yet somehow life just seems to get more complicated, more busy. And, in the end, we're not very happy. And we feel like we've failed. Like we've missed something everyone else has figured out. Like we're losers.

We're not.

It wasn't until I took a look at my life and realized how unhappy and anxious I'd been feeling, how unhealthy I was living, and how distant Hubbie and I were becoming that I decided that the notion of having it all is just bogus. Only then did I decide to cut myself a break, to make changes that wouldn't just get me back on the same old track…but onto a new, blissful one.

And I decided to reach out to those around me—women and men—to do the same. Together, we embraced the fact that the problems of juggling work and our responsibilities and our partner and our children and (gasp!) our own personal needs had to come with a different set of answers.

Those answers are what this book is all about.

HOW I WROTE THIS BOOK
My Qualitative Search for Bliss

When I started telling others about my idea for this book, a few things happened.

First of all, lots of people said they didn't just want to read it, but that they *needed* to read it. Immediately. They were struggling and drowning and downright unhappy because they couldn't figure out how to achieve a balanced life…one that really meant something to them. One that truly fed them. One that made them happy.

The second thing was that I knew I had some extra work to do because I was nowhere near an expert on the subject. Unlike my previous books, where I'd lived the lessons—often painfully—and come out on the other side with some wisdom, this time around I knew I'd need some help. Sure, I understood well the ramifications of falling into the idealized notion of work/life balance and subsequently falling on my face...but I wasn't yet quite sure how to overcome the challenge and find bliss. True bliss. And so I set out to find people who I believed had figured this out.

What I *didn't* do, to be clear, was engage in a quantitative study, complete with surveys and representative samples and lots of spreadsheets. That's just not my style and it's not what I believed I needed for this project.

Instead, I took a more qualitative approach, doing what I always do when I want to learn something new. I figured out who already had it figured out and then asked them how they did it. Instead of engaging in scientific research, I engaged in what I call *bliss-search*.

I began by scouring through my list of colleagues, friends and loved ones. I went all the way back to my teenage years, considering everyone I'd remained in touch with in some way. One name at a time I went through a list of thousands of people, considering my experiences with them, what I knew about them, the way they carried themselves and the way they communicated.

As I considered the list and identified people I wanted to interview, I wasn't necessarily focusing on people who were balanced. Instead, I looked for people who were happy. For real. Then I asked them how they balanced out their lives to get there.

After all, this is about being blissful. That's the end goal. So that was the goal of my search.

Finding those who seemed happy every once in a while wasn't good enough. My criteria involved finding people who were calm while also being driven. The people who had grace under pressure despite their challenges. The people who took things in stride. The people who had an uncanny ability to *not* take things personally. The people who were pleasant to be around. The people who thrived in their own skin. The people who smiled a lot…and whose smiles were real.

To be honest, there weren't tons of people on the list who fit all of these criteria. But when I found them, I immediately knew they were the ones.

These people gave me hope. Hope that it's possible to be happy *and* successful. Hope that even though life is about making tough sacrifices, sacrificing *happiness* isn't necessary. Not at all. They'd proven it. They were blissful. And I wanted to find out how they did it.

In the end I identified 29 people representing different genders, ages, generations, sexual orientations, races and geographical regions (though all were within the United States). They included entrepreneurs, academics, employees and stay-at-home parents. They represented a wide spectrum of professions, management/leadership levels, interests and experiences. A few were interviewed as couples. Some were interviewed as participants in focus groups. Their responses, tidbits and wisdom are featured throughout this book.

(*Note:* When I attribute a quote or story to a person, I describe the person in one of a few ways, depending on the context. Sometimes I get specific about a person's occupation, and sometimes I don't list it at all. There are also times when I stay more general, distinguishing between someone who works for a business (employee) and someone who owns a business (entrepreneur). You will find that many of the quotes and stories come from blissfuls who are in their 50s, 60s and 70s, which makes sense since these wise individuals have had more time to learn their valuable lessons.)

To be clear, these blissfuls did not lead charmed lives. They suffered just like the rest of us. Some had gone through divorces and some had lost loved ones to illness. Some had been—or currently were—sick themselves. Many were under tremendous pressure in their jobs. But they were also blissful. They didn't dread their days or their nights. As I described earlier, they liked their lives and the people in them. They had a sense of continued, underlying happiness, of what they called pure joy.

Sounds pretty amazing, right? I thought so, too.

And so I decided to figure out what got them there.

In addition to my 29 blissfuls, I interviewed a few from the other side—people who, it seemed, were decidedly *not* blissful. These people were always racing from thing to thing, usually breathlessly and with a frenetic energy. They talked a lot about being overworked and overtired. They tended to take things personally and didn't crack quite as many smiles. They were also known to compete with and gossip about others. In the end, they just weren't happy in their lives. And I decided to figure out what got them there.

To round things out, I conducted a brief survey that I distributed to a women's group to which I belong. I also conducted two brief focus groups with women from this group. There were no requirements to participate and they could opt in only if it interested them.

For those of you who like some numbers with your words, here's the breakdown of my interview subjects:

- Blissfuls interviewed in focus groups: 12 (two groups, six per group)

- Blissfuls interviewed one-on-one or as a couple: 17

- Non-blissful interviews: 3

- Women's group survey respondents: 52

- Women's group focus group participants: 9

Grand total: 93 people

In the end, this was not about a broad set of data. This was about targeting. This was about those few people who had figured out how to be happy despite their trials, tribulations and wild rides in life…and who had tales to tell about how they got there. This was also about hearing from others who struggled, about identifying the challenges in particular that made the journey to bliss so difficult.

And, in the end, this was about helping all of us get on that blissful journey once and for all.

HOW TO USE THIS BOOK

As you get ready to begin your blissful journey, there are a few things to know about how this book is designed to help you get there.

First, this book is actually part workbook. Which means, obviously, that it will require some *work*. But don't let this deter you. Work isn't just about putting forth lots of effort. It's certainly not about putting forth lots of effort and getting little in return.

Instead, this work is meant to be meaningful, thought-provoking and—dare I say it—even fun. After all, this is all about figuring out what will balance your life for real, what will leave you feeling relatively blissful a whole lot of the time. This is about discovering what truly makes you tick, and then planning on how to get more of it. My hope is that you'll pursue your journey with a sense of excitement, with a sense of curiosity... imagining how you'll feel when you've gotten to the end, when your life is truly balanced, truly blissful.

The book includes three primary sections. Section I is all about *Breaking Down the Bogus Part*, exploring the whole notion of bogus balance and how we make things worse for ourselves without even knowing it. It's not as much fun as the other parts of the book, I'll admit, but it's important. We all need to face some facts. And, if it makes you feel any better, we *all* have a way of making our situations worse before we make them better. Plus it's the shortest section in the book. So don't skip it!

Section II gets you down to business by *Building Up the Blissful Part*. This section is where most of the *work* in the workbook comes in. It's where you'll learn a whole bunch of lessons from those who have found true, honest-to-goodness bliss, and then dig into it yourself by taking those lessons and creating your own blissful plan. It contains a number of *Bliss Builders*, interactive exercises that are filled with reflective questions that will help you contemplate your current life, your future (more blissful) life and the changes you will make to get from one to the other. The exercises may be filled out on your own, or you can visit *www.bogusbalance.com*, where you can print the forms or access our interactive worksheets.

You probably won't want to complete this section all in one sitting. Instead, I recommend that you give this section a good amount of time, energy and thought, creating some breathing room and mulling it over throughout the process. Complete each chapter by responding to the various *Bliss Builder* questions on a separate piece of paper or your computer, then contemplate for a bit of time. Reflect. (This being said, if there is a chapter in this section that doesn't pertain to your life at all, you may want to skip it.)

Now, while I highly recommend using this book in the way I described above, which is to work through the exercises and create your blissful plan, it is also possible to read the chapters in Section II without completing the activities. Just know that the blissful lessons contained in this section won't be nearly as helpful or powerful if you don't plan how you will integrate them into your own life.

On to Section III. What you'll learn pretty quickly through this book (and what you already know, I'm sure) is that getting to bliss will require some change, which just might freak you out. Which just might convince you to get right off of the bliss train and back to what you know…even if it's unblissful. That is why this section is all about *Battling Those Sneaky Bliss-Busters*. It's jam-packed with ideas, tips and tricks to keep yourself—and that sometimes critical mind of yours—on track.

In-between each chapter of the book you'll find a *Bliss Bit*. The *Bliss Bits* are the definitions of bliss, straight from the mouths of my blissfuls. Though the goal of this journey is to get to and continue a blissful life, and while we can all understand what bliss means to a point, what's also become clear is that specific definitions and nuanced ideas of what bliss actually means vary from person to person. Your own definition of bliss will be unique to you. And while chances are bliss will not be the primary emotion *all of the time*, you'll still feel your bliss as a consistent underlying emotion, one that you can carry with you throughout the day.

The point is that bliss—no matter how it's defined—*is* possible. And worth all of the work to get there. The *Bliss Bits* are meant to help you remember this throughout the process, to give you a continued sprinkle of light, reminding you of what awaits you when you achieve a blissful life. When I asked my blissfuls to define bliss, their responses came in two forms. Some described the *feeling* of living a blissful life, while others summarized what their blissful life is composed of on a given day. I've included both kinds of answers.

The end of the book contains an appendix, which is a *Bliss Builder* worksheet for your ongoing blissful check-in. (It's also available at *www.bogusbalance.com*.) I recommend completing this document three to four weeks after you finish the book, then again every few months in your first year. You may then wish to return to it regularly in subsequent years as you feel yourself evolving or returning to an unblissful place. I also recommend doing what I do, which is to conduct a total blissful checkup by completing *all* of Section II at least once each year.

So, ready to get started?

Good. Because you're about to do so right now.

At the same time that you are reading this book, I encourage you to engage in your first *Bliss Builder* exercise, which is to keep a very brief journal. Or log. Or diary. Whatever concept will help you feel most energized and least overwhelmed. No eye-rolling, please.

This exercise is very important. In order to reach bliss in the future you must first understand where you're starting from. You need to get a sense of how you feel today. You must get a sense of what's working and not working for you. This journal will help you track your current days and the bliss (or lack thereof) in them. It will be one of the tools you use to create your blissful plan down the road.

Take a look at the *Bliss Builder* exercise below and commit to logging your answers for at least as long as it takes you to reach Chapter 9, where you'll use it to create your blissful plan. If you're truly taking your time with the book, then it should be enough time for you to get a good picture of your current situation. If you plan to quickly read through the book in a few days, you'll still want to do this daily check-in and use the information you've gathered once you get to Chapter 9. In that case, you may also want to continue the logging process for another two weeks, using your updated reflections to evolve your plan over time. (Note: This journaling exercise is another feature available at *www.bogusbalance.com*.)

BLISS BUILDER EXERCISE
What's the deal with your present life?

Wake up five minutes early and reflect briefly on the hours ahead of you. Answer the following:

1. Which parts of the coming day fill you with enthusiasm and positive energy?

2. Which projects, tasks or people coming your way make you sigh with displeasure?

At the end of the day, look back at your day and ask yourself the following:

1. In general, what was your energy like today? Why?

2. What parts of the day did you enjoy the most? What left you the most energized and excited?

3. What parts of the day did you enjoy the least?

4. Who specifically contributed to your positive energy?

5. Who specifically brought a negative experience?

Let yourself just observe your day and respond to these questions without judging. There are no right or wrong answers here. You might feel guilty when some of the things that drag you down are the things that you (or others) believe you *should* be doing…or when certain people end up as more of a drag on your energy than they are a boost for you. No matter. This is about you and your bliss. You need to be true to yourself. And everyone else who may have an opinion? They can butt out.

Okay, you've got your first assignment.

Ready to move on? Of course you are!

To Section I…

BLISS BIT

"To me, bliss is the ultimate state of happiness, joy, personal fulfillment. I saw it yesterday on the face of my grandson who was celebrating his second birthday and had just bitten into a large icing-covered cupcake. That smile, those eyes, portrayed ultimate joy and happiness."

Section I

BREAKING DOWN
THE BOGUS PART

SO HERE YOU are, all ready to get moving through Section I. Terrific!

As a reminder, this section will explore the bogus balance phenomenon. It will help you understand just what bogus balance *is*, and why so many of us get so bogged down in it.

Even though this section might be a bit less, shall we say, positively energized than the others, it's an extremely important set of chapters. It's critical to understand the factors behind bogus balance because it will help you avoid pitfalls later, once you're officially on the journey to bliss. It will also remind you that you are not alone in your bogus situation. At one time or another, all of us find ourselves overwhelmed by life, perhaps a bit paralyzed by the multitude of obligations and commitments in any given day. It's not a fun feeling, but it's common. And so learning just how it happens—often when we're not even paying attention—will help you avoid it in the future.

We'll begin this section by digging a bit deeper into the work/life balance concept and why it's such a setup for stress and unhappiness. We'll then take a look at how we all make the whole situation more bogus, exploring the cultural and environmental norms, not to mention the habits we create for ourselves that keep bliss out of reach. Finally we'll discuss the "bogus bottom," the phenomenon that causes many of us to finally change our tune, to finally turn our lives toward bliss.

So, enjoy Section I. There's a lot of good stuff in there. And take a minute to thank yourself for doing what you need to do to explore this issue. Your efforts will help you find true balance. They will help you find bliss. In the end, you and the people around you will be so glad that you did.

CHAPTER 1

The Problem with a Name

"Work/life balance? I'm offended by the phrase itself."
—BLISSFUL MAN IN HIS 50s

THE FIRST THING we need to get down to is the problem with the "work/life balance" label. Over time the whole concept has become completely false, leading many, many of us to keep ourselves mired in all of that bogus muck. Unconsciously, of course.

And the problem begins with the name. Actually, there are a few problems with the "work/life balance" phrase. Let's dig a bit deeper...

1. THE WORK/LIFE SPLIT.

The first problem with this phrase begins with the separation of those two little words: *work* and *life*.

When interviewing my blissfuls, I found that many of them said they resented the idea that work is separate from life. It insinuates that life is something we live with passion, something we're here to enjoy...while work is something we do to attain that passion. It insinuates that work is the toll we pay to enter the highway of life. And so it insinuates that work doesn't need to mean anything or be especially enjoyable.

Instead, my blissfuls stated confidently that work is a *part* of life, something they love just as much as the other parts. The notion that life didn't begin until they'd stepped out of the work box wasn't just wrong. It was offensive.

My blissfuls said—without guilt or judgment—that when you find what you love to do and you do it wholeheartedly, work is just as much a part of the richness of life as spending time with your kids or being on vacation. It can be just as enjoyable, just as fulfilling and just as frustrating as all the rest of it. (Let's face it, they said: that big, pressure-filled project *and* that trip to Disneyland *both* have their ups and downs.)

Replacing the words *work* and *life* with *professional* and *personal* gets closer to defining life's various categories. No matter what, they're both part of your *life*. Every part of your life must be chosen carefully, for the right reasons. Every part must be lived with energy and intention. My blissfuls have figured this out, and found ways to create a life where all components feed and fulfill them. They've found ways to live the whole shebang with a purpose, grace and—yes—bliss.

One of my blissfuls, a CEO in his 60s, put it this way:

> *"You can't separate your job from your life. You won't be happy and you'll always be angry about work going into personal life...versus hey, it's your life, it's all of who you are. I know I do good things at work and make a difference all the time. So I accept it and then enjoy it."*

The thing I appreciated most about this discussion wasn't just the fact that the blissfuls wanted their work to be as fulfilling as everything else, but that they were so unapologetic about it.

It's funny how so many of us are trained to love certain parts of our lives (such as our families) best, while liking the other parts somewhat but not nearly as much (such as our work). Not so with my blissfuls. Work was a critically important part of their blissful lives, often just as important as, and a few times even more important than, anything else. And they were proud to say so.

2. THE LIFE STEW: TODAY'S TECH REALITY.

My search of the phrase "work/life balance" showed it was first used in the United Kingdom sometime in the 1970s. It was created to illustrate the fact that we have different portions of our lives that need focus, and so we need to figure out how to balance them.

What this conjures up to me is an image of one of those old TV dinner trays...one where there are isolated components of our lives. These components each have their own, neat little place. No messiness, no overlapping.

Perhaps in those early years of the phrase it was easier to separate our work and our personal lives from each other more neatly. Perhaps we could close the door on the office at the end of the workday and travel to our homes, where our families awaited us. We could shut down the first part and enter the second part, and the two would never need to meet. It was certainly rare for the two to bleed into each other. Sure, we might get a phone call saying there was an emergency at work or at home and we needed to address it. But this kind of overlap of the professional and the personal was more of the exception. Separation was the rule.

To be honest, I don't suspect that this idea of separating work and personal elements of our lives made people happy even then. It certainly didn't seem to help them find fulfillment or bliss. I was around in the 1970s and remember plenty of unhappy people. At the same time, it does seem that keeping the two components of work and personal life separate was easier to do, and so people did it. Right or wrong. Happy or not.

Today, of course, things are very, very different. Which makes complete separation of our work and personal lives impossible.

Today most of us are pretty much accessible to pretty much anyone at pretty much any time. Smartphones and texting and social media have made us reachable anywhere, whether in our offices, sitting at a beach or flying through the skies.

Gone are the days when we could shut down one portion of our lives so we could focus fully on another. Gone are the days when reaching over the TV tray barrier to get the attention of someone was an exception instead of the rule. Gone are the days when we had to assess whether an emergency from the other side was truly big enough to break our focus from what we were doing at that moment.

As times have changed, so have our perceptions of both our time and the time of others. Our time is no longer strictly for ourselves and our families. The continued and rapid rise of technological advancements have locked us together in cyberspace, always there with each other—if not in person, then just a few button pushes away. Being accessible at all times has become not just a standard, but a sign of our world's digital success.

But social expectations have moved beyond simply being accessible all of the time. Now it seems we're expected to *respond* whenever we are accessed. At whatever time of day, no matter what else we might be focusing on.

Got an email from the boss about a new company policy that needs reviewing? Better do it tonight or risk giving the message that your job isn't a priority. Received a text from a colleague saying she had a horrible day and wants you to join her at a happy hour across town? Better respond soon or risk giving the message that you don't care.

Somehow, focusing our time and energies strictly on the component of our life that's right in front of us is no longer possible. Instead, we have traded in true focus for a rapid flicking of our attention from thing to thing, a buzzing and roving of our minds over all of the items that demand our attention at any given moment. And so our focus is split up into teensy little pieces...from Word document to email to the online site where we buy our favorite shoes, all in a 30-second stretch. Sometimes we attend to it all while we're on the phone. Or driving. Even when we sit down to tackle a big project with a major impending deadline, we keep our phones close by and our inboxes open. Just in case. Even when our tech is shut off, our minds are still fluttering about, thinking about what might be awaiting us there or the people who may have reached out to us.

It has become nearly impossible—and very rare—to give all of our energy to one thing at one time these days. Sitting at our kid's music concert while texting a colleague is not just a regular occurrence, but also widely accepted. We think we're getting it all done in the way it all needs to get done. But what's really happening, if we're going to be honest, is that when we're doing both things at once we're doing both of them partly well...and partly poorly.

And here's the other thing, since we're being real.

In today's world we're not just accessible to people all the time...and we don't just feel we must be responsive to them.

We *love* to be.

We'll talk more about this in the next chapter, but for now I just ask that you keep yourself open to this idea. Even if your shoulders tensed and your mouth opened in silent protest at this notion, please lay down your defense mechanism on this point for a just a few more minutes.

All of this is to say that the whole work/life balance notion—the one of neatly separated, TV dinner tray components—is completely bogus. Instead, our lives are one big, messy stew, all mixed together so that work edges into personal stuff and personal stuff edges into work.

It's not necessarily a bad thing. It's not necessarily a good thing. It's just the reality of today.

Our task, therefore, is to figure out how to find a sense of balance and peace despite that reality.

3. THE CRAPPY THING IT INSINUATES.

We touched on this in the introduction...and it's the fact that just using the phrase "work/life balance" insinuates that it is *possible* in the first place.

It's not. At least not in the way we've always heard about it.

Work/life balance tends to be connected to the notion that it's possible to do *everything*—to take advantage of every single opportunity and play every role available to us—very, very well. It means that when we work, we do more than just get it done. We excel at it all the time. It means that when we're with our kids, we do more than just assist them in becoming stable, happy adults as best we can. We become super-parents along the way. It means that, when it comes to our relationships, we don't just spend time with our friends, partners and loved ones. We are there for them all of the time and we are there for ourselves all of the time. We are emblems of support, love and grace. All of the time.

We are promised that if we just balance everything correctly, nothing will be ordinary. It will *all* be extraordinary. *All* the time. In every part of our life, personal and professional.

Bogus.

One of my non-blissfuls blames this notion of having it all on the additional pressure she feels every single day, and the way it makes her feel as a result:

"It's a survival feeling, not a happy feeling. I'm so busy with both work and kids, and don't feel like I do anything well. I always feel like I'm putting Band-Aids on things, like I'm just keeping my head above water. It's almost impossible to achieve balance. I've slowly learned I can't have it all, but I don't feel like I can do anything about it right now. I'm stuck. So I've accepted it. But do I feel blissful or at peace? No."

Perhaps you can relate?

But the stories don't end there. As part of my bliss-search I conducted a brief survey with 52 women, all of whom were members of a co-working space to which I belong.

As part of the survey, I asked them to name the greatest challenges they've experienced in striving to achieve work/life bliss.

A long and varied list of answers came in. In no particular order, here's a small sample:

- Managing my work schedule with my other full-time job: my kids

- Feeling guilty about taking downtime

- Worried that if I don't spend 80% of my time working on my small start-up, I won't keep up with the competition

- Focusing less on the money and more on creativity

- When my kids are home from college and my routine changes

- My husband wants more attention and my 82-year-old mother needs help

- Cleaning the house

- Having "me" time

- Feeling that time spent at work is ineffective/inefficient

- Getting distracted

- Going to school and working at the same time

- Unplanned events that require immediate action

...and the list went on from there, illustrating the fact that many, many of us struggle daily with the bogus balance phenomenon.

The notion of having it all if we just find a little bit of balance has got to go. Instead, bliss needs to be looked at differently—starting with the decision *not* to have *it all*. Instead, bliss is about figuring out *your all*...what really matters to you, what's feasible, what—in the end—will delight you. Bliss is about being discerning. About making choices to have certain things in your life *instead of* other things.

Yes, there will be sacrifices when you choose *your all*. But, in the end, *your all* will be comprised of the things that delight you the most, the things that feed you the most, the things that make you blissful...the most. The best part is, unlike having *it all*, achieving *your all* is indeed attainable.

One of my blissfuls, a retired high-ranking academic, tried to have *it all* for a while. Until she realized she couldn't...which is when she realized she had the power, the right and the need to make choices. Here's how she put it:

> *"I had been teaching for a few years, and after I had kids I tried to keep on doing it. But I realized I couldn't be a mom and be at school...and give 100 percent to all of it. That's when it hit me, and I don't care what anybody says—you can't have it all. When we had our second child, my husband and I decided I would stay at home*

and just be Mom. *I felt happier, and I loved seeing my kids grow up. To be honest, we were totally broke when we went from two salaries to one, but we knew that was our choice so we didn't regret it. Realizing that I couldn't have it all set the right course for me for the rest of my life."*

An important lesson, but a tough one. Because it involves sacrifices. It involves choices. But, it also involves true balance. It involves bliss.

Letting go of the idea of having *it all*, and determining *your all*, is one of the most important things you can do to overcome bogus balance. Yes, making hard choices between the things in your life might sound so much easier said than done, but the important thing to know is that it *can be done.* Promise.

You'll get there soon. And then you'll go farther.

BLISS BIT

"I think that most people think that bliss is to have hours a day to pamper, meditate, cook the perfect foods, read all they want, etc. NOT ME! I like having to manage my schedule and commitments, make time for exercise, sometimes having to eat a protein bar because there is no time for a proper meal, etc. Idleness is my true enemy. For me, a blissful life is to be busy doing good in the world, interacting with interesting and ethical people, having fun. Bliss is also having manageable challenges that can be conquered. Bliss is feeling loved and respected in my community, and doing for others as well."

CHAPTER 2

How We Make the Whole Thing More Bogus

"I officially suck at relaxing."
—NON-BLISSFUL WOMAN IN HER 30s

AS MUCH AS we might prefer to point fingers at people and situations in our lives for making things so incredibly unbalanced and non-blissful, the discussions with both my blissfuls and my other interviewees actually cleared up the identity of our biggest enemies in this regard:

Ourselves.

In our quest to achieve bliss, we get in our own way…in lots of ways. It turns out we are our own worst adversaries.

Now let me say here that this is not something that just a few of us do. We *all* have an uncanny ability to get in the way of our own bliss. Every single one of us.

There is nothing wrong with us. In fact, we can find perfectly rational, logical, sometimes passionately believed reasons for messing things up for ourselves. The problem is that our self-sabotage actually works *so well*. Which means that along the way, as we get in our own way, we become unbalanced, stressed out and unhappy. And we feel trapped in our misery.

I include below just some of the ways we botch up our own bliss. It's a diverse list, but the underlying theme centers around a simple concept: the choices we make.

Or the choices we don't. Or the choices we pretend we can't.

What's hard to swallow for many people is that we have more choices than we think we do in our lives...including choices around our schedules and work. Even *not* making a choice means you are making a choice—to either let others decide your level of bliss for you or just to stay stuck in general.

You'll see what I mean as you begin reading through the list.

1. WE SCAM OURSELVES ABOUT TECHNOLOGY.

Okay, let's get down to it.

I brought this up a bit in the last chapter and I asked you to remain open. Ready?

As we discussed, our email inboxes, texting conversations and social media channels are no longer simply a convenient way to stay in touch when we need to do so. They now represent an *expectation* of constant accessibility and communication. The *dings* signaling new arrivals in our inboxes are constant interruptions, constant focus-breakers and constant intruders into every part of our day, both professional and personal... whether we need them or not.

And, if we really think about it, we've grown to like it. Actually, most of us have grown to love it.

Think about it. There's a reason that we tend to jump with a somewhat adrenaline-like start when we hear that digital ding or ring or buzz that means someone has reached out to us. There's a reason we put everything else down to see who it is.

When someone contacts us—especially when it's off-hours from our usual time together—that means we're needed. It means we're important. It means someone is thinking of us. And, as a bonus, it means we've got something to distract us from our buzzing thoughts or the things we don't want to do at the moment.

The ding is like a wrapped gift that hasn't yet been opened. It represents something new to us, a mystery, even for just that moment before we find out who and what is behind it. After all, in the seconds it takes us to locate that phone and look at that screen it could be anyone. About anything.

Despite our collective whining about being constantly disturbed and inundated by technology, despite our efforts to convince ourselves and others that we constantly check our tech when we're out of the office strictly to keep everything cleaned up when we're back in it, for many of us technology has become the thing that keeps us feeling sane. It's our mechanism to check in, feel connected and feel important.

I'm not saying this in judgment, especially since I also get the ding-related buzz regularly. I'm saying this because we need to be real about why we keep the phone on over dinner or during that big meeting.

Yes, there might be an emergency. Yes, the boss might need us for something big. But, chances are, the majority of whatever we receive in our beloved little technological devices can wait— even for a little while—so that we can focus fully on our current situation. We just don't think about it that way. Nor do we necessarily want to. Because, let's face it, adrenaline is kind of nice.

What I want to emphasize here is that despite what we want to believe, *we make a choice* about this. We allow this to happen. And then we make excuses as though we don't have a choice. We do.

If you find yourself constantly checking to see who's responded to your latest social media post or jumping at the sound of your texting ding, then fine. But be honest with yourself about why you're doing it. Know that it's not just about being there when it's important, but just being *there*…being accessible and available whenever anyone shoots any bit of information your way. Know you do it because it feels good to be needed or wanted…or just to be in the game. At all times. Instead of where you are right now.

Know how much that part of you that wants to be important and loved and included is running the show.

And remember, you're not alone in this. No judgy-judgy here. We all do it. We all love it.

2. WE DON'T SET LIMITS.

One of the bliss barriers I heard over and over, especially from my women's group survey responses, was people's lack of discipline in setting limits—and the stress and self-hatred related to it.

While some of the examples I received on this issue had to do with parents struggling to set limits with their kids, most of the responses were related to respondents' career paths. Those who had bosses would bend over backwards for them, never saying "no" because they didn't think they could. Those who ran businesses would bend over backwards for their clients, never saying "no" because they didn't think they could. Or because they just felt guilty when they weren't working on their business in some way.

Exhibit A: The following social media post I happened to run across recently. It was posted by a female entrepreneur on a Sunday (she subsequently gave me permission to use it here):

> *"The biggest problem with having a job where you don't have to clock in is it's impossible to clock out. I'm so trying*

to give myself a break and not work today but I don't think I'll last too much longer. I can hear my laptop calling my name from the other room."

Just what is behind our continuing struggle to set limits within our life stews?

There were several themes identified by the respondents:

- Many were terrified that saying no once or setting limits would suggest that they weren't committed, and would result in them being less respected in the future. As a result, they made choices *not* to set limits with those at work...while limiting the time spent on their personal life-stew components.

- Many said the fact that technology is always on means that they could be...and always should be...on as well, or else risk seeming like they didn't care (see previous point). They said having no finite end to technology meant having no finite end to the workday... which meant the amount of time to get things done and move ahead is actually *infinite*. And to get ahead they needed to take advantage of that.

- The other, lesser-spoken but striking, sentiment was that those struggling with setting limits didn't think they could prove themselves *any other way* than by pounding out work at all kinds of hours. Some seemed to believe themselves that they actually weren't worthy unless they metaphorically killed themselves to show how committed they were. These people convinced themselves that setting limits for their own lives was not an option. Underneath it all was the underlying sense that they needed to prove themselves as valuable to others because they themselves didn't necessarily believe in their own value...and until they proved that value to all involved they didn't deserve to have a life outside of work anyway.

Another theme tied to a failure to set limits had to do with the lack of an ability, or desire, to delegate. Both the women and the men I interviewed recognized that one of their biggest bliss barriers was their need to do everything themselves.

And boy did they come up with all kinds of reasons for this. Some said their standards were just too high to trust others to do something that they were involved in. Others said they just loved being part of the game and wanted to keep working at all times. Others didn't feel like they should delegate because they didn't want to inconvenience others with something they themselves could do. And as we've already heard in other contexts, many said they felt better doing everything because they felt this proved their worth.

One especially honest woman, an organizational leader in her 50s, talked about the fact that she never delegated because she needed to believe that she herself was irreplaceable...that nobody could do the work like she could. She also said that, sometimes, delegation was a forgotten concept altogether:

"I'm the biggest barrier to this...I say yes to too many things so work can eat me alive. Sometimes I just forget to ask others to help me, and sometimes I'm not even aware of the option in my mind."

3. WE BEAT THE CRAP OUT OF OURSELVES.

Wow, are we ever good at this one.

We're our own worst enemies because, in a lot of cases, we treat ourselves like garbage. We say things to ourselves with that inner voice of ours, things we would never say to others we respected or cared about even a little.

When things go wrong, it becomes about our flaws. When things go right, we often believe it's circumstantial. We got lucky.

When things go wrong, we beat ourselves up for not trying hard enough or for failing to give it our all. When things go well, we barely notice them—and certainly don't celebrate them—before moving on to more pressing issues.

Beating the crap out of ourselves reflects that we think doing so is okay, that we deserve it because…somehow…we believe we are crappy. Beating the crap out of ourselves reflects our low self-esteem, our low sense of self-worth. And the only way to prove we are worthy is to be successful—and perfect—in everything we do. Even though that's impossible. As one of my interviewees, an entrepreneur in her 60s, told me:

> *"My own head is my greatest challenge. It's my own critical self that gets in my way. Failure is emotionally horrible for me. I always feel I fail when my company struggles."*

On a personal note, this particular issue has become a major sticking point for me. When the people around me do this to themselves, it drives me crazy. When I hear people beat themselves up—which is all the time—I feel caught between wanting to hug them tightly and smacking some sense into them (my apologies to you pacifists). Yet I do it to myself all the

19

time, of course. Which is why we're in this together. And why we're going to stop doing it as best we can.

Right?

4. ENTER...THE GUILT MONSTER.

Oh, that guilt monster. It's a tenacious little bugger, popping up all the time, in every part of our life stew. And it completely screws up our bliss.

This problem came up for many, many of my interviewees, and it's a messy one.

Guilt is that constant feeling in the pit of our gut that we aren't doing anything well, and that we're letting all kinds of people down as a result. Women in particular, especially the ones in my focus groups, talked a lot about feeling chronic guilt...about not giving enough to their work, not paying enough attention to their kids, not looking out for their mothers and siblings and best friends. Interestingly, they didn't seem to feel bad about the lack of care they gave to *themselves*. Instead, that was just part of the bargain. (This gross misconception will be tackled in Section II.)

For many of us, the guilt monster appears *whenever* things don't go exactly as planned. Whenever we don't do as well as we wanted to do. Whenever we don't get everything done. Whenever we feel others are disappointed in us or we've let them down because we haven't been perfect. Whenever we feel we have said something, done something...even thought something that wasn't *right*. Somehow imperfection becomes about us and our lack of skill, commitment, integrity...you name it. We convince ourselves that whatever happened was because we didn't try hard enough, weren't smart enough, didn't care enough. And it's so bogus.

Wanting to be perfect is like wanting to turn the sky green. It's just not possible. We know this about others. Yet, for some reason, we think perfection is possible for *us*. We give ourselves special, incredibly high and unreachable standards about everything we do in life, from our jobs to our yoga poses. And when we're not perfect—because we can *never be perfect*—we don't just beat ourselves up. We also feel like we've let the world down, disappointed others, not been our best. It's a terrible, recurrent tune we sing in our own heads. Often we don't even know we're doing it because it's become such a common part of our mental song. It is paralyzing, taking over our thoughts, distracting us from what we're trying to get done...never mind all of the good we're doing along the way. Simply put, the guilt monster must be slayed for bliss to be achieved.

If this describes you, trust me when I tell you that you *can* slay it. More to come on this, but for now, on to...

5. WE TELL OURSELVES BOGUS STORIES.

Stressful or unhappy situations happen all the time. The problem is that we allow ourselves to stay stuck in them. We stay in jobs we can't stand, stay in relationships that don't work, choose other people's priorities over our own on a regular basis.

How do we allow this to happen? How do we become the perpetrator of these bogus circumstances?

We tell ourselves the perfect stories to justify it all.

We know ourselves well and we know how to convince ourselves that we have no other choice but to stay right in the unhappy situation we're in. Even when we know we have a choice, we tell ourselves stories as to why we must stay with the disagreeable, sometimes miserable option.

We get specific with our stories, manipulating what we know to be our sensitive spots and playing on the arguments we know we'll believe. We tell ourselves we can't leave our miserable job because it would be irresponsible to quit when our son is only in his second year of college. We tell ourselves we must stay just a bit longer at the office to finish our project (while our partner is waiting for us at home) because we might just get that promotion if we prove ourselves. We tell ourselves we can skip our favorite book club meeting, the one that we love so much, *again*, because we need to update our company's website before our clients all go somewhere else.

We tell ourselves sleep is overrated. We tell ourselves we'll eat healthier tomorrow. We tell ourselves now is the time we must push ourselves…that we will relax later, that we will spend more time with our loved ones as soon as things calm down at work, that we will work on our relationship just as soon as our kids start high school and aren't so needy.

We push ourselves toward more stress and away from things that feed us. We tell ourselves that this is what we *must* do right now. That we are responsible adults. That now is not the time to be lazy or selfish or…*fill in the blank.*

Perhaps, deep down, we tell ourselves we don't deserve the happy stuff. Not yet, anyway. Not until we've earned it by…*fill in the blank.*

And it works perfectly. We then believe our stories all the way to our core, throwing up our hands to the inevitable reality that we've created in our imaginations.

Why do we do this? Because our stories allow us to avoid conflict, to avoid discomfort. They allow us to avoid the fear that comes with change. They allow us to just stick with what we know simply because *we know it*, even if it makes us miserable.

It makes perfect sense, really. Fear is a very powerful thing. So is uncertainty. Most of us don't want either in our lives, so we do whatever we can to convince ourselves to stay right where we are, even if it makes us unhappy. Which is why the bogus stories we make up are so amazingly good.

I heard lots of stories like these in my bliss-search. One non-blissful woman explained to me that she can't see her pre-teen daughters as much as she wants to because of her need to work harder and prove herself in her new position:

> *"You can't have the job I have at the level I have, at the salary I have, and the expectations and responsibility that come with it, and have equal time to focus on family and health. The good thing is I have an inner understanding of my kids, which helps me know what they need from me at any given time, even if I don't see them as much as I'd like to...I've set some lofty goals and so have rationalized in my head that this is the way it will work."*

Can you hear the bogus-ness in her story? Chances are you can. But that's because it's not your story. Chances are you've got your own stories, and chances are they are just as bogus.

The good news is that's about to end.

6. WE NEGOTIATE. POORLY.

Sometimes the stories we tell ourselves take on the specific form of negotiation with ourselves. It's a tactic many of us use when we feel conflict between our work and personal lives, or between what we *want* to do and what we *think we should* do.

I heard this throughout my bliss-search. Here's a specific example. Two separate interview participants, a male entrepreneur and a female employee, both in their 40s, knew that they worked far too many hours. They both knew their schedules could not be sustained if they wanted to be in happy relationships or be healthy in the long run. They both said the same thing, which is that things could not continue in this way. And so they both negotiated a deal with themselves.

I was struck by the fact that each made the same exact pact, which was to allow themselves to continue this way for five more years. Just five more years, each of them said. After that, they both said, they would feel satisfied taking more time away from their professional lives. They'd feel ready to find better boundaries, settle into a life filled with more time with their families, and find a better sense of overall wellness.

Five more years. It had better not be more than that, they said. In fact, the male interviewee provided his own warning to himself: "Man, if I am still at this pace in five more years…"And then he stopped. He had no idea how to end the sentence. And so he just shrugged.

For many of us, negotiating with ourselves comes with the bogus notion that we need to *earn* happiness…that we simply cannot allow more time to enjoy our lives until we've achieved that title, that salary, that perfectly completed project. Even little things like taking a walk during our lunch break are not allowed until we've earned it by answering all of our emails. Which, by the way, never happens.

That word, *earn,* is a dangerous one. We're big believers in *earning* the good stuff. And we negotiate that the other, blissful stuff will happen only once we do. The problem, of course, is that we never feel like we've done enough to earn it because there's *always more to do.* And even when we do what we said we would, we move the bar higher and higher, always fearful that we could slide at any moment, lose our successes, lose the respect we've worked so hard to earn. Which means all those better, happier things we imagined, the things we've always told ourselves we were fighting for, stay in our imagination forever.

We need to learn how to use *earn* the way the word is meant to be used...for things like an academic degree or a salary or someone's respect. We need to unlearn this habit we have of negotiating our bliss until we've earned it.

Because we've all earned it already, just by being here on this planet. Some might say that living a blissful life is part of what we're here for in the first place.

I end this chapter the same way I began it—by talking about choices. Here's one of my favorite interview quotes, from a non-blissful organizational executive who is drowning in the thick of his work as I write this. He told me that finding his own bliss continues to be a regular struggle. And he knows the truth about his role in it:

> *"You are your own best advocate and worst enemy when it comes to this stuff. It's not other people's problems. People bash their job or boss as though they are to blame for their unhappiness. But in the end I think you have to say to yourself 'I can make some choices in the game.' You don't need to get a lawyer and sue your boss because work eats up your time. It's the company's intent to eat up your time. It's up to you to figure out how to get your work done, keep your business relationships strong and also keep your personal life in check."*

Well said.

BLISS BIT

"To me, a blissful life is a life where you experience simple moments of pure and natural joy. A moment where you forget all that you need, forget all that you want and forget the cares or worries that exist in your life. These moments are simple, unforced and easy to take for granted."

CHAPTER 3

The Bogus Bottom

"It's like a crisis is almost necessary and inevitable."
—BLISSFUL MAN IN HIS 70s

WE'VE GOT ONE more thing to cover before moving onto your official path to bliss.

It's about something I discovered only once I started my bliss-search.

It's what I call the bogus bottom.

Here's how it works.

When it came to interviewing my blissfuls, the stories I heard weren't just about their current states of bliss, but also about how they finally achieved them after living non-blissfully for years. Their journeys to bliss always included some tension, some mistakes and—in most cases—a whole lot of pain. Many blissfuls talked about the start of their paths, how they were unbalanced, filled with conflict.

They talked about being stressed all the time. They talked about losing friendships because they never made time for those they cared about. One person told me he was a terrible parent.

But then something happened, and they got to bliss.

And I realized there was a theme to how they got there, the thing that finally helped them come to terms with the fact that they weren't happy, that they would need to change. I realized there was a common thread that led most of these blissfuls to their bliss: the bogus bottom.

It turned out that before these blissfuls could reach their bliss, before they even realized they needed to get on the path at all, they had to hit some kind of bottom. A bottom that was drastic enough that it shook them at some level, gave them perspective, propelled them from their less happy, more bogus lives, to a new path…a more joyful path.

Many of us have heard of the phrase "hitting a bottom" in the context of recovery from drug addiction, alcoholism or other life struggles. It means that a person will continue whatever the unhealthy behavior might be until something happens that is so bad that he or she decides to change. Until change is the only option. Until the person hits bottom.

But bottoms aren't isolated to those who find recovery. They're something many of us can relate to, something many of us need to reach in order to create positive change in our lives.

It's not enough to be told life is short, that you need to simply be true to yourself and remember what's important (though we will get into these points in a bit). It's not enough to just know at some level that nobody is perfect and so we need to ease up on ourselves. Because as much as we believe it about others, we tend to think that we're the special ones. That we *are* perfect. That we're untouchable by tragedy and disease and divorce.

And that's how it went for these folks.

Until the tragedy happened. Until someone got sick or got divorced or lost a job or had a breakdown of some kind.

Now, these bottoms were different than just a bad day or two. The bottoms my blissfuls experienced included challenging, painful and/or life-changing events that caused them to stop in their tracks and decide to make a change. It led to that "aha!" moment. It motivated them to turn their lives around, to make new choices, to aim for bliss.

Some had a high bottom, something relatively mild. These bottoms included the beginning of marital problems, a slip in health, the realization that they were unhappy in their jobs after a screaming match with the boss. One said her bottom happened after she had her first child and realized that leaving her baby every single morning was making her absolutely miserable…leading her to reprioritize, change her schedule and make sacrifices so she could be home more. These fortunate high-bottom people didn't suffer too much pain or tragedy before realizing they needed to change, that they could find better bliss.

Others weren't so easily convinced.

Many of my blissfuls had a family member get very sick or die. Several experienced one or two divorces. A group of them—those who tended to have more intense, A-type personalities—became ill themselves.

One example stands out for me. It came from my very first interviewee, a retired executive in his 70s. I'd known him for just a few years and always found him to be extremely centered, balanced and happy. He was the perfect fit for my blissful criteria.

I also knew that his past *wasn't* so blissful…that he had been more intense in the past, that he'd been more aggressive in life. When I asked him what had happened to get him from there—aggressive and tense—to bliss, he said the following:

> *"I'd say it had to do with an open-heart surgery, a back surgery, several knee surgeries and a gallbladder surgery…"*

I sat up straight as the idea of the bogus bottom first flashed into my brain. I wanted to learn from him, to figure out how to help others prevent their own nasty bottoms if possible.

So I asked him expectantly, "How could you have gotten to this blissful place sooner, without all of that suffering? What could have happened, what could have been said or done to get you to realize that things needed to change before you went through all of that? Before you hit such a low, difficult bottom?" I leaned in for the answer excitedly, expecting a grain of wisdom that would prevent so many people from so much unhappiness.

And then he looked me straight in the eye and said without hesitation:

"Nothing."

I sank back in my chair. Nothing?

When I pressed him on it he said that everyone is on his or her own path, that it's not about hearing about other people's stories or learning the statistics of what happens to super-stressed-out, super-miserable people. Too many of us just don't believe such things will happen to us.

Too many of us don't even think it's possible, frankly. And too many of us think that we're so special that we don't have the luxury of making the same kinds of choices about our lives, the ones that will truly make us happy, that other people do.

And so what I had to accept is that almost everyone will hit some kind of bottom before making real change. And that bottom will be different for each person.

I understand the bogus bottom because I hit my own…the potential ending of my second marriage. When it came to a head, when the "D" word actually entered our vocabulary as a possibility, I thought it was the biggest problem I had…the thing I needed to fix.

And while there were plenty of issues to work out between us, it turned out that this bottom was just a symptom that shined a big spotlight on the other issues in my life that were keeping me from being blissful (such as the need to succeed in my business at all costs, the pressure I put on myself, the constant anxiety I was feeling, the unhealthy ways I treated myself).

In the end, the bottom was a blessing, because—as painful as it was—it got me on the journey to bliss. It didn't just save my marriage, it saved *me*. It helped me turn everything around, to make better choices before the bottom got even lower.

So, really, the bottom isn't necessarily a bad thing since it gets you on track. But it seems that the sooner you get there, the higher the bottom that you hit, the better.

So the question, of course, is how low will your bottom need to be before you change?

The thing that gives me hope for you is that you're reading this book, which may mean one of two things. First, you may have already reached a bottom and are now ready to put it behind you and find a happier life. Or…perhaps you sense that you're approaching a bottom, and want to get on a new path before you get there. Either way, you're here because you want to get to bliss. In fact, you're darn well ready for it. And so you're willing to learn the blissful lessons, put them to use for yourself and reach bliss.

So let's keep going…and help you get there.

BLISS BIT

"For me, bliss is about excitement.
There's always excitement."

BUILDING UP
THE BLISSFUL PART

WELL, LOOK AT you...all set and ready to roll at the start of Section II. Excellent!

Now that you've gained a bit more clarity around bogus balance, let's get down to the true goal, yes? Which is to get you on your path to bliss.

This section addresses the various parts of your life stew. It contains specific lessons and stories from my blissfuls, who can explain firsthand how they created *their all*, how the choices they've made in life have led them to true balance and real bliss. It will also give you the chance to take those lessons and apply them to your life so that they work for you. After all, your blissful life will not be a duplicate of anyone else's, but will be unique to you, creating a stew that makes you feel energized, fulfilled and happy.

The first several chapters in this section (chapters 4 through 8) explore some specific stew components. We'll begin with a look at the blissful career, which will be followed up with explorations of the blissful life partnership, the blissful family, the blissful others and the blissful you.

Each of these chapters will end with a *Bliss Builder* exercise, a set of questions designed to get you reflecting on your current life, and how you will bring it to a new state of bliss.

Chapter 9 will give you the chance to take what you've learned, reflected on and explored, and integrate it into your own, customized plan for happiness…a blissful blueprint, if you will. All of the exercises may be filled out on your own, or you can visit *www.bogusbalance.com*, where you can print the forms or access our interactive worksheets.

There are a few things to consider as you prepare to embark on this section.

First, I encourage you to commit to responding to the various *Bliss Builder* exercises with as much honesty and self-reflection as you can. Many of us have gotten good at judging ourselves, or feeling like we must do things a certain way because others tell us we should. Let's be clear: this is about you. So take the time to make the best blissful blueprint for you, and let yourself be the *you* that you want to be. After all, you're the one who will be living this life when the work is done.

I'd also like to ask that you give this section some time. There is no need to speed through the entire section in a day. It's a good idea to complete a chapter or two, then take some time to breathe and further reflect, perhaps going back to your earlier reflections and adding some further thoughts.

Finally, I invite you to go about this section and this process with positive energy and curiosity. Yes, it takes time. But it can also be fun. It's a time to play and explore. It's a chance for you to dream, to look ahead to what will make you happy, to imagine your future blissful life

Okay, enough for now. I invite you to plunge in with Chapter 4 and your blissful career.

CHAPTER 4

The Blissful Career

---

*"My work has to make me happy if I'm going to
spend the majority of my time doing it."*

—BLISSFUL WOMAN IN HER 30s

SO HERE WE are, all ready to explore the blissful career.

It's interesting. When I first identified my list of blissfuls, I expected that part of their bliss would be attributed to a schedule that included working less, which then helped them make time for their families and the things that were important to them. I thought it would be all boundaries all the time, that they'd found clean, clear ways to set work limits for themselves and mined the discipline to heed them.

As much as I believe in the "life is a messy stew" concept, I somehow thought their stews would be a bit...neater. And I thought the pieces would be skewed toward their personal components, that their personal passions would be larger, would completely dominate somehow.

I was wrong.

Most of my blissfuls, it turned out, worked *a lot*. When asked the percentage of waking hours they spent on work, the majority figured it fell between 70 and 80 percent. A few of them said it was 100 percent because they were always thinking of new ideas and strategies related to their work ("I even dream about work at night," one of them said without apology).

But, because they'd made certain choices, it was all worth it. In fact, their careers were *part* of their blissful life stews. All of the time and energy and, yes, frustrations that are a part of any work situation were all worth it in the end. Well worth it.

One note here: The career paths of my blissfuls included everything from traditional office positions (representing all levels, including the top CEO dog) to entrepreneurial business ownership to project-based contract work. And while I use the word *career* in this chapter, my bliss-search also included responses from people who intentionally chose *not* to pursue a specific career path, often working part-time positions and focusing on raising their families instead. No matter what the parameters of the work, my blissfuls were clear in their universal themes, and in the specific strategies and wisdom they used to make the professional components of their stews as blissful as they could be in order to feel that sense of joy, fulfillment and peace of mind that mattered so much to them. That matters so much to all of us.

By following the lessons below and the ones found in other chapters, my blissfuls could rise each morning with a sense of happiness and curiosity…and a noticeable lack of dread. They could end each day tired, but satisfied with how it had been filled. They knew that every minute they put into their work was worth it because on the whole it made them happy, because it left them feeling satisfied, because it created energy and enthusiasm, which they then carried to other parts of their lives. By following their blissful lessons, my blissfuls successfully created *their all*, and they loved it. All of it. They smiled more. They laughed more. They didn't sweat the small stuff and they handled the big stuff with grace. They didn't just live their lives, but *loved* to live their lives.

Not too shabby.

1. FIND THE FIT.

When it came to finding the right work component in their stews, my blissfuls were all about quality over quantity.

These people said that a major factor in their bliss was due to having chosen (yes, *chosen!*) work that truly fulfilled them, work that they valued because they believed it served a purpose, made a difference, stimulated them, used their skills in a worthwhile way...all along the way achieving goals that mattered to them.

Temptations to take a job solely because it paid the most or offered the more impressive title were resisted. Instead, my blissfuls found jobs and careers that they truly *enjoyed*. They searched hard, finding positions that felt naturally aligned with their interests and skills, that fit both what they were *able* to do and what they *loved* to do.

When my blissfuls found themselves in a position they didn't like, they changed it. They didn't necessarily do it immediately, but they changed it as quickly as they could. And they didn't tell themselves a whole list of bogus stories to keep themselves stuck.

To again be clear, their work lives weren't perfect (nor were their lives in general). Every job has its stresses and downsides. But because these blissfuls had jobs they truly loved, jobs that fed them, the stress was often easier to deal with. The cost/benefit analysis related to their happiness came out positive.

This all might feel so obvious to you. It did to me, too. But here's the difference. My blissfuls didn't just believe it was important to find work that you love...they insisted on it with an unwavering commitment. They settled for nothing else. Having a job that made them blissful always won out when they made their career choices. Nothing else mattered as much. Not their egos. Not their fear of change. Nothing.

One interviewee, a television executive, illustrated my point, though I'll admit he also surprised me. I didn't have him down as a blissful when I set up our interview, and the reason was that he worked more hours than anybody I know. In fact, when we spoke, he told me he spent about 90 percent of his waking time either in the office or outside of it analyzing and thinking about his work. And so I thought he must be stressed, unfulfilled, incomplete.

Not so, because the work was such a joy for him. Here's what he said:

> *"Amazingly I am perfectly fine with my percentage. I always knew what I wanted to do and now I'm doing it. In fact, I actually still get a kick out of the fact that I'm paid to do it at all."*

And he said it with a smile.

I realized that just because his work component in the stew was so much greater than mine didn't mean he wasn't happy. He made his choices about his stew very intentionally. He'd found a mix—and a specific career—that worked for him, that gave him joy. And that's the whole point of this journey.

Even those blissfuls who didn't always find themselves in the perfect job at the moment still had a way of making their experience positive until they could change it.

A blissful CEO in his 60s said his bliss was about knowing that any job he found himself in gave him the chance to do his best, make a difference, and enjoy the ride:

> *"Even back when I was a kid cleaning bathrooms, it was always about how I could make my job better, more interesting, more efficient. I always appreciated getting to know the people around me because I got to find out what they were like and what they were trying to accomplish.*

*And I always had fun. Even today I am constantly think-
ing about the work I'm involved in. It makes me happy to
make a commitment to do a job as well as I possibly can,
and then to know I'll do it."*

Whether you agree with their specific statements or sentiments,
the important theme from these blissfuls is their attitudes about
their work. They found work they loved and they did it from a
place of bliss. Pure and simple.

Not easy, necessarily, but pure and simple.

These blissfuls knew that one of the greatest benefits of finding a blissful career path is that when it did indeed blur into
the personal components of their life's stew...when they found
themselves having to work late to meet a deadline or answer
a call from a client while at home...it was okay. In fact, it was
a part of their joy. Because their job wasn't an obligatory slog,
but something that brought them happiness, something they
looked forward to. Every day.

And when that stopped, they changed it.

Sometimes the change wasn't due to stress, but simply due
to the fact that the blissful felt he or she had moved beyond the
position. It became tedious and boring, which was unacceptable.

I interviewed one blissful, a high-level employee in her 60s,
who had announced her departure from her position and was
in the midst of her transition. Here's what she had to say when I
asked her why she chose to make a change:

*"The job has become too easy. I feel like I've done it all.
Plus, after some changes at the office I'm surrounded by
mediocrity and it drives me crazy. I don't ever want to get
tired of my job, so I've had to think about what I'm going
to do next. And now I'm going to do it."*

By the way, you might already know all about the importance of choosing the right job, and find your struggle is in figuring out just what kind of work will actually make you blissful *in the first place.*

If this is the case for you, don't worry. We'll get to that soon. Hang tight.

2. AVOID THE "BAD BOSS".

Another very important theme for my blissfuls was their refusal to settle for a "bad boss."

This one might not be so obvious. Since our very first job, many of us have thought that the boss is just a part of the professional package, something we need to accept. And that's certainly true to an extent. We can't all have the perfect boss. In fact, none of us can. The perfect boss doesn't exist.

This being said, the boss can also make or break your level of bliss at a job. The seemingly best job in the world can turn pretty terrible pretty quickly when the person who has authority over you treats you differently from the way you want to be treated.

My blissfuls didn't always love their bosses, nor did they believe it was necessary to do so. But they did insist on a relationship where they felt respected, where they got the support they needed and where they were able to both perform at work and have the time, space and energy needed to live the other parts of their lives the way they wanted to live them.

They avoided the "bad boss" because they knew it was critical to their bliss.

Here's how one blissful, a retired employee in his 70s, described his "right boss" mentality:

"Who you work for is critical. When you work for some-one you respect and who respects you back, someone you can be honest with, fight with and disagree with...some-one who gives you authority when it's right to do so, that's what works. When you can't have that relationship or those discussions, your work can become very difficult."

It's that simple. Bliss at work includes finding the right boss. For *you.*

Think about it. If you need independence and a boss is a micro-manager, then you'll be miserable. Often. If you need a lot of support and your boss is never around, then you'll be mis-erable. Often. If your boss takes things out on you or treats you like garbage for whatever reason and this kind of behavior frus-trates you, then you'll be miserable. Often. And no matter how much the job itself feeds you, you'll still be miserable. Often.

(By the way, my blissfuls involved in business entrepreneur-ship—who didn't have a traditional boss—followed the same kind of rule with their clients and with the staff they hired. They knew that a positive work experience relies as much on the people who surround you as anything else.)

When the boss relationships weren't working out, my bliss-fuls addressed it professionally and head-on. Often the dis-cussions led to solutions. Sometimes not. In these cases, they knew they needed to find new answers—new jobs or different positions within a business—in order to find the relationship that worked for them. It wasn't a question of "sucking it up," of sticking with a boss who constantly impacted their work neg-atively, in order to keep their lives stable. It was a question of being blissful.

One of my blissfuls, who wanted a good career but pri-oritized her family time higher, didn't stop looking for a job until she found the right boss for her...someone who respected family time as much as she did. She said that to this day, her boss actually gives her a hard time if she's at her desk after 5 p.m., so there's never any guilt or conflict around getting home on time. And that makes those rare occurrences when she does have to stay a bit late perfectly fine for her.

All because she chose the right boss.

Now, how is it, you might be wondering, that I could use the word *chose*? After all, we don't really have a choice in the matter of our bosses, do we?

Of course we do! And it is up to us to make sure it's the *right* choice. Before we agree to take any position in any company, it is up to us to have a good one-on-one with the person who will manage us. It is up to us to (respectfully) ask the right questions to find out what the boss's expectations are. It is up to us to have determined beforehand what our needs are around being managed, what kind of communication and support we need, what kind of boundaries we need when we are not in the office...and to find a job and boss that fit our needs.

Remember, times have changed. We are accessible virtually all of the time. Just how much of this time will you be expected to be responsive? To be working? As you make choices about your career path, know your potential boss's expectations. This won't just help you be happier, but will prevent certain boss-related pitfalls before they happen...the kind where you play games like sending emails late into the night to show your boss you care...the kind where you find yourself struggling with whether or not to answer a call from your boss at dinnertime. Discussions and clarifications now will make sure that you can make choices that are true to you later.

(Sure, there will be times when you need to work outside of your ideal hours, but be careful not to establish patterns of communication or work that aren't what you're looking for. Patterns quickly turn into expectations at work.)

We cannot settle for a boss we know will be the wrong fit, one we know deep down will make us miserable…who will turn that incredible job into a miserable experience. We have a say in this. And if we don't make the best choices for ourselves, nobody else will.

Despite what many of us were brought up to believe, and also how it feels when we're on the job hunt, a job interview isn't a one-way sales job. It's a two-way conversation. And if you don't get a good vibe from the man or woman who will have management authority over you each and every day, then you should think again before accepting the job. No matter what the money. It's not easy, but it's important. So make every decision carefully. Your bliss may be at stake.

What if you're in a position right now and dealing with a "bad boss" situation? Do what my blissfuls do. Change it somehow.

Find a solution. Have a hard but respectful conversation about what you need and see if it can be worked out. Know that some dynamics don't always work and determine if yours is too much of a hindrance to your bliss. Get creative about new positions or dynamics that might be better for you. Ultimately, just know that you have a choice in this. Even if it might be painful at first.

Again, this can be hard, painful stuff. It's not easy to consider leaving a job that provides security and a salary and opportunity. And yes, there may be times when those things need to win out for a while. But, in the end, if your relationship with your boss is making all of that good work stuff rather sour rather regularly, then considering your options and creating change is important. After all, nobody likes a sour life.

3. YOUR TITLE, YOUR SALARY, YOURSELF.

I've alluded to this point already, but now it's time to get explicit. Because it's very important.

It's about that ever-important title. That ever-important salary. And how they both relate to that ever-important sense of self.

Or do they?

I know from my own experience how much a title can matter, and how it can influence our choices. I felt it strongly during the moment in my journey when I left my somewhat impressively titled position to start my own business and take on a decidedly less popular title: *consultant*.

After hitting my bogus bottom it all became crystal clear to me...the reasons why I had allowed my business (and making it as successful as humanly possible) to take priority over everything else. Which caused so much damage to everything else.

I let it happen because I didn't know how to value and identify myself anymore. I no longer had a title I could be proud of. I could no longer impress others with tales of working my way up and around various professional ladders in a company. I no longer got up at a certain time to go to a certain office and achieve a certain thing in order to earn my certain title and salary.

And because I had lost all of these ways to identify myself, I *had* to make sure my business succeeded. At all costs. Because that would now be the way I proved my worth...to others. To myself.

Every decision I made about how I spent my time focused on my business first. In a way it felt like my very survival relied on it. After all, if I left all of the previous things that identified me in order to start my business and it wasn't good enough, then just who was I? Why did I matter at all? At that point I just needed to be relevant...being happy didn't come into the picture at all for me.

Finally, as I fell flat on my bogus bottom and the rest of my stew began to fall apart, I realized just how unhappy I was. I realized how deeply I'd let my own ego, my own issues of self-worth, get in the way of what really did matter.

And that's when I realized the truth...that a job or a business is a *part* of a person's life, an important part, but not all of it. I realized that a title is a label to help explain what we *do*, but it doesn't define who we *are*.

We are who we are, which is lovely and messy and ever-changing. We are worthwhile because we are here in this world and because of the people we decide to be. Not because of what we do. Or what we earn.

And that's when I made a change. I reprioritized, began making decisions that actually made me happy. I still worked a lot of hours because I truly liked running my business, but I didn't work *all* of them. And—in a turn of events that admittedly surprised me—my business profits went up despite my shortened workday. My goals were still achieved. And I was able to do it by enjoying my work as I went, not going about it in a breathless, intense way that sucked all of the life out of every effort because so much—my very identity—was riding on my success.

I considered this issue when I prepared my bliss-search, and developed a hypothesis as to how the ego would (or would not) play into the lives of my blissfuls. I guessed that my blissfuls would certainly value their titles and salaries, but that these things wouldn't be *everything* to them.

In this case they proved my hypothesis correct. When I carefully asked them to rank the value they placed on their titles from 1 to 10, more than 80 percent ranked it below 5 (only two blissfuls said their titles came in at 9 or 10). One woman, a retired superintendent of a school district, said she used to "chuckle at it."

To be clear, these blissfuls were proud of their work and what they'd achieved. They knew their titles got them access to opportunities and they were grateful for that. But they didn't believe their titles defined them as people...nor they did get impressed by the titles of others.

One of my blissfuls, a journalist in her 50s who was somewhat of a local celebrity at one time, was very clear about her title's importance (or lack thereof):

"My title was never a big deal to me. I don't care what other people know about who I am or what I do. I'm certainly proud of what I do, but if I meet someone new I don't necessarily introduce myself by my title. Being a minor celebrity didn't give me a rush. What gave me a rush was making a difference and doing a great job."

I heard a whole lot of comments to this same effect. My blissfuls knew how to keep their egos in check. They didn't feel the need to throw out their titles to anyone who would listen just to prove that they were valuable.

They already knew they were.

As a result, they were able to make solid decisions about how they spent their time, focusing on priorities that made them blissful—which sometimes meant lots of time spent on their professional careers and sometimes meant lots of time spent on other things. They were able to go about their decision-making from a place of self-assuredness and self-value… without the burden of feeling like focusing less on work would make them less valuable as people.

My blissfuls also knew there was another danger related to valuing a title so intently in their lives: the fact that it will be gone one day. A CEO in his 60s put it like this:

"I believe I've been fortunate to get my title, and I know when I leave, chances are the world will forget me...so I can't let it mean anything. What's really important is what you do with your work and what you mean to the people around you."

So if titles didn't matter all that much to my blissfuls, what about their salaries?

It turns out that the blissfuls looked at money in a similar way. It mattered, certainly, but it didn't define them any more than their titles defined them.

More than 90 percent of my blissfuls said that money was important only because it allowed them to provide for their families and/or contribute to their communities, which made them feel good.

An interesting point came from one blissful, a nonprofit organizational employee in her 50s. She said that one of the most important changes in her career came when she left a job that paid a relatively high amount for one that paid significantly *less*, but that also allowed her to follow her passion in the nonprofit world. It not only made her more blissful, but also came with an unexpected benefit: even though the change meant sacrifices for her and her family, it also taught her children the difference between want and need...a critical lesson that they still carry with them today.

Again, these points might seem obvious. But what's clear from my discussions with others who aren't quite so blissful is that many, many of us struggle in making and living the choices that lead to bliss. We struggle to find jobs that don't just feed our financial and ego needs, but that we actually *like* over the long term. For some reason we feel we need to sacrifice true, pure *enjoyment* in our jobs in order to get our other life needs met.

We don't. We can have both. We can find the right position, career or business opportunity for ourselves...the one that pays the bills *and* makes us happy. We can keep up our search until we find it. We can work hard and feel good about it. We can be happy at the beginning *and* the end of the workday.

My blissfuls did. A female executive in her 60s summed it up this way:

> *"It's always been my nature to work hard, but I love it so I'm happy. I have a passion for the work I do. I enjoy it, and I feel good about it. I actually don't have to do it anymore, but I like this company, the people and the mission. I work for the people we serve, and I believe we continue to make a difference."*

BLISS BUILDER EXERCISE
Your Blissful Career

You've now reached your first set of interactive *Bliss Builder* exercises in Section II. Welcome!

These next few chapters contain some questions designed to get you to reflect on *your all*...your life stew and what you need to be happy. They will help you assess what is working or not working for you right now, as well as what might help you be more blissful in the future. Remember that you can either fill out all of the exercises on your own or visit *www.bogusbalance.com*, where you can print the forms or access our interactive worksheets.

In addition to this series of exercises, you will want to continue the logging exercise described at the start of this book as you work through this section. You will use your log, as well as your responses to the reflective questions in these next few chapters, to put together your more specific blissful plan in Chapter 9.

And please remember that these exercises are meant to create positive energy. So dream. And have fun. This is good stuff.

We begin here with some questions related to your blissful career. This section will allow you to reflect on your current path, assisting you in determining what may or may not be working toward your bliss. If you are in a situation where you are not on a career path but want to be, or want to change it to something else and need to figure out what that something else is, we will get to that soon.

Let's begin. Take a pen to paper or boot up that computer and answer the following questions. Remember that nobody will see this but you, so answer honestly and without judgment. There are no *shoulds* here. This is about you and what you honestly feel. So write your answer and move on before you can talk yourself out of it (please note: for questions that ask you to rank 1 to 10, 10 is the highest or best).

1. In general, how do you feel when you wake up in the morning and look ahead to your workday? Is this acceptable to you?

2. In general, how do you feel at the end of your workday? Is this acceptable to you?

3. On a scale of 1 to 10, how much do you enjoy your current profession? Is this number acceptable to you?

4. What parts of your profession do you find yourself most looking forward to?

5. Approximately what percentage of your work time do these activities take up?

6. Which parts of your profession do you decidedly dislike...perhaps dread?

7. Approximately what percentage of your work time do these activities take up?

8. What kind of relationship, support and communication do you have with your boss? Is this acceptable to you?

9. On a scale of 1 to 10, how important is your title to you? What does it mean to you?

10. On a scale of 1 to 10, how important is your salary to you? What does it mean to you?

11. How would you feel if you woke up tomorrow and had a title and salary that you felt were less impressive? How would this impact the way you felt about yourself?

12. Is the above answer acceptable to you? If not, what are some ideas you have to increase your sense of self-worth?

Now, keeping in mind your responses above and noting the themes, complete the following sentences:

In general, the blissful parts of my current professional path are:

In general, the negative parts of my current professional path are:

In general, I believe the following changes will create a more blissful career path:

Alrighty then…first set of exercises complete. Nicely done!

We now move on to another critical bliss element: your primary partnership. Of course, if you feel the need to first take a break and reflect on what you've already read and done, by all means please do so. It's most important that you give this process the time and energy it deserves…because that's how you'll get the greatest bliss that you deserve.

I'll see you in Chapter 5, when you're ready.

BLISS BIT

"In my case, a blissful life comes in moments, not years. It means time with a partner I love, opportunities to truly be a mother to my kids and a grandmother to theirs, the kind of good health that allows me to ski all winter and cycle all summer, great vacations in wild places, and a sense of true accomplishment in my professional life—if not every day, then often enough to feel proud of myself."

CHAPTER 5

The Blissful Life Partnership

---

*"A day rarely goes by when one of us
doesn't make the other laugh."*

—BLISSFUL MAN IN HIS 60s

I BEGIN THE chapter on your primary life partnership in a way that might surprise you.

I begin it by letting you know that some of my blissfuls said the role of a primary partnership in their lives was…none. These individuals clearly stated and believed that the existence of a partnership isn't always necessary to achieve bliss. Some of them made the intentional decision *not* to be in a primary partnership and they were perfectly happy with this choice. Their priorities included their work or business, their friends, their extended families. Some decided a partnership would mean sacrificing too much of what they themselves wanted. It's a new way of thinking for many of us, but it's important to understand that the lack of a partnership doesn't mean a lack of bliss. In fact, for these people, the lack of one contributed to their bliss.

Now, all of this being said, many of us *do* want to include a primary life partnership as part of our life stews, and this is also a perfectly fine choice. It's all about what will create *our all*, right?

(Note: The word *partnership* as it is used in this book is intended to denote the primary romantic relationship, including a marriage, live-in situation or other relationship where two people live their lives and make family/household/financial decisions together.)

For those blissfuls who did have life partners, their life partnerships mattered. *A lot.* In fact, they believed that the primary partnership can make—or break—the level of bliss in one's life.

If you have decided that having a primary partner is a priority, then chances are you understand the power this kind of partnership has in your life.

This power is not about domination or authority. It's about the way it shapes your day, the tone and energy it brings to your activities, the level of happiness or frustration you experience within your own home. After all, partners have chosen to live in an enclosed, often small amount of space with each other for an extended period of time. Often the partner is both the physical body and the mental energy that's next to you when you first arise…and when you officially end your day. And, because it's a *partnership*, compromise is the name of the game.

A partnership can be a very tricky thing. Think about it. You and your partner were brought up in different households, learning different ways to be, speak, think, interact, show affection, spend money, raise children, practice spirituality and look at the world. At some point, you and your partner have decided (or you and your future partner will decide) to live in one place and blend your two very different life cultures, hoping that you will have the interest, patience and communication skills to understand how these two cultures are influencing everything you both say and do. At some point you will then use that understanding to make decisions about your lives, and perhaps the lives of your children (should this be another priority you make in your life. If so, we'll get to that in the next chapter).

The power of your partnership is that it is always *there* in some way. Even an absent partner has a hold over you, because he or she is in your thoughts and therefore using up your energy. It may be positive. It may not be.

Despite the fact that a healthy, happy primary partnership may be an obvious factor in achieving bliss, a large number of the people I spoke with continually struggle to actually find one. Many have settled into an unhappy pattern or relationship, have lost hope that true bliss is possible, have told themselves stories about why they can't make change.

Not so with my blissfuls.

By now we've learned that they don't settle. In the last chapter we learned that they don't settle for an unblissful career, and here we learn that they won't settle for an unblissful relationship...one that's more of a hindrance than a help in living a blissful life. And because they don't settle, they've sometimes had to make hard choices...and changes...to get there.

The partnerships my blissfuls found weren't easy all of the time, but they had a sense of *ease* about them. The love wasn't forced. The arguments came and went without resentments. Laughter outweighed clenched, frustrated fights. They looked forward to their time together.

Heck, they liked each other.

One blissful, an entrepreneur in his 60s, described his partnership as his number-one priority, over both his work and children. He believed the experiences with his life partner were what made his life so blissful. "After all," he said, "you can't have a glass of wine with your job."

These partners didn't need a lot of communication or debate back and forth every time there was a need to work a bit late or miss out on one of the kids' soccer games. The partners were there for each other, acting out of love and support first.

A big reason was that these partnerships included two people who had their own levels of self-confidence and worth, and who knew how to get their own needs met...so they were able to find delight in loving and supporting the other. They were able to root for each other in every part of life—the parts that included each other and the parts that didn't.

Again, no partnership is perfect. But when the blissful times and the not-so-blissful times were weighed against each other, bliss came out on top. The majority of the time my blissfuls felt supported the way they needed to be, felt stimulated, loved and honored the way they needed to be. The majority of the time, they felt an intense need to reciprocate. And, throughout it all, they were able to be exactly who they were. No exceptions. No apologies. No judgments. They knew this would make them happy.

And they were indeed happy. Because they weren't just in partnerships, but pleasant, positive, smiling, energetic ones. These blissfuls authentically enjoyed each other's company. A blissful woman in her 50s described her partnership this way:

> *"I've always felt like a torpedo rushing home at the end of the day—like I couldn't get home to my husband fast enough. I just couldn't wait to get there so we could live our shared world together."*

Easy enough to achieve, right? Of course not. But I did spend a good amount of time talking with my blissfuls about how to get there.

And boy, did they have some counsel in this area. Like so many of the rest of us, my blissfuls had learned a lot through both happiness and pain. Their ideas and stories are like light posts on our paths, giving us guidance and ideas and hope...the hope that our partnerships don't just need to be about having an additional salary to pay the bills or an extra hand to raise the kids, but are also about providing affection, support, fun and... ultimately...bliss.

Before we get to some specifics, I do want to interject with one important note.

While your partnership does hold a tremendous amount of power around your bliss, ultimately your level of bliss is up to you. Bliss ultimately comes down to how happy you are with yourself, how loving you are with yourself, and how much you value yourself. The best way to have a healthy partnership is to be a healthy partner yourself—one who knows how special and lovely you are before going into the relationship. When you know this, you will not need to derive those things from the other person...who may never be able to give you the exact words you need to feel valuable because he or she simply doesn't understand your needs the way you do.

So now that we've gotten that out of the way, let's get to wisdom from our blissfuls, shall we? Again, it's important to understand that these points didn't just lead to a somewhat good life, but helped them create a *blissful* life. It meant that the primary partnership was far more delight than problems, far more pleasure than pain. And it contributed to a life stew that left my blissfuls feeling energized, supported, loved and...well...just plain happy. Not all the time, of course, but a whole lot of it.

1. FIND THE RIGHT FIT.

Sound familiar? Yep, this first step reflects the same sentiment as the first step in finding the blissful career path. Finding the right fit...for you.

It's all about figuring out what you need and want, deciding what you need to make you as blissful as possible, and then intentionally finding the right fit to get you there.

This fit will be different for everyone, of course. You, like everyone, have different needs, want different things and function differently than everybody else. Which means you need to find the right partner—and the right way of conducting your partnership—for *you.*

The first step? Taking the time to think through just what your needs are. Just what will make you happy regularly? What level of support do you need? What level of affection and intimacy? What kind of communication works best for you? What kind of personality? What kind of sense of humor? What matters?

A blissful high-level CEO in his 60s who valued his life partnership, but who also strongly valued his work, knew he needed to find a partner who would be okay with his intense focus on his job. And so he did:

> *"We'd go hiking and I'd get a cell phone call and have to go back to work. I brought laptops on vacation and there was never any problem. She had no resentment. She just always knew who I was."*

The sentiment above is not everybody's idea of a blissful partnership, perhaps, but that's not the point. The point is that this couple found the partner that worked for each of them.

As you think through your blissful list, remember that your right fit will not—cannot—be perfect. But you need to know what matters most. You need to know how you want to feel when you're with your partner. You need to know what a blissful day with your partner—which will hopefully be many, many days—will look like.

You also need to know that, chances are, your right fit will not be a mirror of you. Nor should it. Puzzle pieces don't fit together when they are built exactly the same. They fit together when certain things missing on one side fill the other to completion.

Again, it's all about finding not *a* partner, but the *right* partner. For my blissfuls that meant finding partners they didn't just love, but who they enjoyed, and who shared similar values. One blissful couple, married for over 30 years and who I interviewed together, put it this way:

> *"For us, marrying the right person has been everything. Even though our personalities are very different, we share the most important values. We are good friends, work and play well together and respect each other, which is so important."*

Like many partnerships, the blissfuls' relationships began with lots of intense romance. But, like all relationships, that passionate intensity didn't last over the long haul. Instead, the romance turned to a stable and functional relationship of love, fun, respect and support.

How? Because my blissfuls made the right choice about who they would have romance with from the beginning. Which created the foundation for that blissful relationship well after those first few months of newly sparked passion.

It didn't always work perfectly the first time. In fact, several blissfuls went through one or more long-term, committed partnerships before they found one that truly worked for them. Several blissfuls actually said they were grateful that they (and, in some cases, their partners) were married before, because it taught them important lessons that they were able to bring to their current partnership.

My blissfuls didn't stop trying until they found partnerships that were authentically caring, loving and filled with support. As with their careers, they knew that making hard choices and, in some cases, hard changes was critical to living a blissful life.

The important thing is to figure out what you need from your partner to be happy, and then to be explicit about those needs in the beginning and throughout the relationship (and I mean *explicit*. Hinting doesn't work).

It's not always easy, especially when one considers it through the lens of balance. Our partner often takes center stage in the personal part of our work/life stew.

After all, when we run late at work, it's our partners who we are impacting and whose ultimate reaction may then impact us. It's our partners whom we rely on to take care of some of the household and childcare needs so that we can participate in our various work functions, creative time and social events. It's our partners whom we must compromise with when making hard decisions about how we will spend the precious time, money and energy in our lives. So we'd better make sure those compromises will work out okay. We'd better find the right fit.

The best-case scenario is to have figured all of this out before you get into your partnership...before the big move-in or ceremony. Yet, if you don't find the right fit in the beginning, all is not lost. The next option is to think about what you need in your current partnership to get you to bliss. You need to decide what changes must be made, which of these changes are possible, whether they are enough to make you truly happy, and how you will achieve them. You need to make your partner a true *partner* in your bliss. And you must be a blissful partner as well.

And once you do, the effort can't stop there. It takes ongoing work and nurturing to keep your blissful partnership blissful. It takes constant understanding, checking in and communication to make sure the needs of *both* partners are being met.

A blissful male entrepreneur in his 60s talked about it this way:

> *"I suffer from a bit of co-dependency, so it's important for me to be honest about what I need. I do this by communication, by being open and honest about where my balance comes from. If I have to work an event, I let my partner*

know that I'm not choosing the event over him, but that I just need to do it. The thing is we are both very supportive of our work decisions. My partner would never ask me not *to choose the work thing. In fact, he'd tell me to do it because he knew it was important to me. He's never given me a hard time. It's just the way we both are, and partners need to agree on these things."*

Finding the right fit and keeping it blissful isn't easy. I myself have been married twice, so I know some things in the area of the blissful partnership. And I know how tough it can be. But I also know how important it is not to settle.

2. UNDERSTAND THE ROLE EACH OF YOU PLAYS.

This next one speaks to the male/female partnership, which relates to some readers, though certainly not all.

For some of my blissfuls this issue impacted their partnerships greatly. It has to do with the male/female role and how our own upbringing and expectations play into it.

In this day and age in which both genders pursue and achieve business success, a few of the women I interviewed pointed out that the issue of gender roles needs to be handled carefully. These women said that their successes have not always been looked on favorably by their husbands, who were ashamed that they weren't making as much money or finding as much success as their wives.

It's important to remember that individuals brought up in certain places and generations have been told lessons and given expectations about being "the provider." Others might just feel pressure to be the bigger earner because it gives them a certain level of security, power or independence. This is not right or wrong; it's just an issue to understand and address.

Understand your partner's expectations and cultural upbringing on the role of men and women, and spend some time truly pinpointing your own. Find a partner willing to support you in the way you need, and who is also willing to communicate his or her own vulnerabilities in this arena. Far too often this issue runs so deep that it isn't obvious until it pops up in all kinds of other symptomatic ways—sensitive disagreements about money and resentful arguments about working too many hours, for instance. Don't wait for this to happen. Understand what each of you believes your role to be, and work out how those beliefs will fit together into the future.

3. PRIORITIZE EVERYTHING...TOGETHER.

Each day will comprise a wide variety of choices about how you and your partner will each spend your time, about how many hours you spend working (including those emails from home or out at networking events), how much time you spend pursuing a personal hobby or attending a group gathering, how much time you spend on the needs of the family and how much time you spend together as a couple.

Before these choices are made it is important for couples to have an understanding from each other about their own, separate priorities, so they can then look at how each will fit into the day.

Knowing both of your professional ambitions and understanding how they will play into a given day is critical. So is understanding each other's personal needs—how much time you each need alone, how deeply you value the pursuit of new skills, how much energy you get by being around your social circle. More importantly, understanding that each person will have *different* values around these areas is critical. Again, there is no right or wrong, no good or bad sets of values. Each person is different and has a right to be.

When you know each other's priorities you can then plan to get your mutual needs met without having it become a personal, emotional tug-of-war each time. You can also plan on how to get the needs of the home met in a way that meets the emotional needs of everyone.

Though many blissfuls said they very much enjoy pursuing hobbies together, some also said their partnership thrives because they allow each other to pursue their own individual interests without it getting in the way...or adding any guilt. One couple told me they even take separate vacations if they really want to experience something that they know will make the other person miserable. These partnerships are strong and secure, made up of individuals who need neither constant attention nor validation from their partners in order to feel good about themselves.

No matter what priorities exist for you and your partner, the important thing to recognize is that each of you has them, and that many will be different. It is important to honor those priorities and talk about how they will be met before they seem to fall away. It is important to bring those priorities into a customized, functional *partnership*, instead of thinking you need to sacrifice everything you love to do in order to make the partnership thrive. You don't. And if you do that, it won't.

Prioritizing together doesn't just have to be about the big stuff in your lives. It can also be about how you plan to spend a given day or week.

A great example came from one blissful who, before she retired, was a school superintendent. She was also married to one. The jobs were both highly demanding on their time. Here's how they handled it:

"Education can be all-consuming if you let it. In our business, school ended at 5 p.m., but that's when sports and other school events began and we were often expected to be there. We began realizing how much it was impacting our time together, and that we had to decide how we would handle it. We sat down regularly to strategize, to figure out where we really needed to be physically. We also planned when we just wouldn't be at certain places. We did it together."

4. THE ISSUE OF RESPECT.

Almost all of my blissfuls used the same word when discussing their functional partnerships: *respect*.

They talked about how important it is for you and your partner to respect each other's needs and goals. They talked about respecting that your partner's needs and goals will not always be the same as yours. Respecting that your partner's life cannot mirror nor revolve around you. Respecting the fact that your partner will find happiness in ways that have nothing to do with you. Respecting the fact that you will need to support your partner in ways that work for him or her. Respecting that everyone is on his or her own path, and that those paths are different.

It means respecting your partner in each of these ways, and also having that respect turned to you in kind.

If you don't respect your partner, how can you have an objective mind when making choices about your day and how you might spend your time most blissfully? How can you focus on raising a family with him or her? How can you keep positive energy and be happy living in a small space with this person for years and years? If you don't respect your partner—and your partner does not respect you and the life you choose to lead—then bliss will be very hard to find in your life.

After all, you want your bliss to *include* a happy partnership...not to exist *despite* an unhappy one. Right?

One of my blissfuls, a woman in her 50s, talked about what she learned from her first marriage, and how she applied it to her second:

> "In my first marriage I deferred to my husband's need for professional satisfaction to my own great expense and personal cost. He definitely wanted what he wanted and I acquiesced. I learned a lot from that. My current husband and I have huge respect for each other's goals and ambitions, so it wouldn't ever surprise him if I had to reschedule our time together for work when I told him the reason. We understand each other's priorities."

My favorite part of the story comes next:

> "At one point he was working on a campaign and was consumed by it. When my birthday came up I made reservations at a restaurant and told him to come and bring his checkbook. I thought, why set him up for failure? I knew he was busy and that I would need to make it happen. People do that when they love each other."

What this woman knew was that she was important to her husband, and that they respected each other. This meant she wanted to be supportive of even those priorities that didn't include her. It helped her *not* take it personally when he was in a place where he couldn't focus on her.

She told me this story about this seemingly small thing with a laugh, but I was struck by it. I couldn't help but wonder...would I have the strength and self-esteem to do something similar without resentment or expectation? Maybe on a good day.

Respect also comes into play in the form of support, which is another critical piece to the blissful partnership. "Support" was another word that came up again and again with my blissfuls.

If my blissfuls were driven to reach certain achievements in their careers, their partners supported it. If they knew there would be times that they couldn't be home because they needed to network or finish a project, their partners supported it. Similarly, one stay-at-home mom said she was able to be successful because her partner knew that she'd need some alone time once he got home from work, and he supported her in that by taking care of the kids.

Sometimes support went a step further, in that some blissfuls actually looked to their partners to help brainstorm new ideas or projects at work. They spent time together finding solutions to challenges that one or both of them were facing in different areas of their lives. While this level of support wasn't a part of every partnership, it mattered highly for those blissfuls who talked about it.

One last point on respect. Sometimes the most important thing you can do to respect your partner is to have a clear understanding of your own stress and mood, and how that might impact the other person. Remember, a home is a relatively small space, and negative energy passes easily around it.

If you're stressed and you need support, that's one thing. But if you're just in a cranky mood from a bad day, it might be just as important to give yourself some space, and your partner a break, until you're through it.

Sometimes you can make a choice to avoid bringing stress home in the first place, either by your attitude or by your schedule.

One of my blissfuls, a male government employee in his 20s, said it this way:

"Sometimes bringing work home means bringing stress home. That's why my partner and I decided it was better for me to work an extra hour at the office every now and then, instead of taking work into the house."

What matters is that these two partners understood each other's needs and made the decision together. And it worked for them.

5. SPEND TIME TOGETHER... AND SET IT IN STONE.

While supporting each other's individual needs was important, my blissfuls were quick to say that another priority must be spending time together. Regularly.

Many of my blissful couples had non-negotiable time together. Examples included a stroll after work each day, a "date night" every Saturday and a time for tea or cocktails when they both got home from work.

The important thing was that it was a regular occurrence. Even the television executive I quoted in the last chapter, the one who spent 90 percent of his time on work, knew that this was important. He and his wife were both in agreement about the work/life stew he'd chosen but they didn't use it as license to ignore their relationship, which is why they spent a dedicated part of the weekend—one of the few times he wasn't working—together. No kids allowed.

In some cases, the time the blissfuls enjoyed together was about the quality of that time—the travel and the special nights out. Yet, while this quality mattered, many blissfuls talked more about the *quantity* of time...that it was long enough to have a true, focused conversation. That is was regular. That it was not to be messed with. Several couples created rituals and patterns in their schedules for things like long walks or chats when the kids went to bed.

One blissful man in his 60s talked about the ritual he and his wife have had for decades, beginning years ago, before he retired:

> *"My wife and I would get home after 5 p.m. and make a cup of tea and spend an hour debriefing. We still do it today and it doesn't have to be deep conversation. We talk about what's going on with our lives and our kids' lives… It's about making sure we communicate. Some stuff is superfluous and less exciting—shopping or sports—but the point is we listen to each other and we connect. It was helpful because once we built up this ritual of communication, it then became easier to talk about the tougher stuff when it came up. But the best part of all of this is that we wanted to do it, because we enjoyed each other's company."*

During this time together set aside by my blissfuls and their partners, there was one other thing (besides the kids) there was noticeably absent.

The tech. Any and all digital devices were off-limits. Phones away. No emailing. No texting. No exceptions.

Think it doesn't matter? It does. True, meaningful, blissful conversations don't happen when partners are paying semi-attention to each other. Semi-attention can begin to feel like you are semi-important very quickly.

To be clear, finding this time wasn't always easy for my blissfuls, who said alone time together was much harder during the years when their kids were young. Yet they all found a way to do it. Some spent time together while actually attending their kids' events. Many just made sure their kids knew early on that alone time for them was going to be a part of their lives, a part that the kids could not interrupt. They let them know this was how it was going to be because they as a couple mattered to each other and loved each other.

A good lesson for these kids to hear at an early age, yes?

In what I found to be a fascinating, perhaps extreme example, one of my blissful couples actually made it clear to their children that their love for each other extended farther than their love for anyone else, including their kids. I followed up by asking one of the daughters (now grown, married and a doctor) how she felt about this. Here's what she said:

> "We always knew this was the way it was growing up. My dad regularly talked about loving my mom more than us. It was actually very reassuring because it created a strong sense of stability. My sister and I knew we were part of a very safe, secure bubble. My parents were always a unit, and that made it easier for us to have structure. It also helped us understand that we could never play one parent against the other. They weren't our friends, they were a united front."

6. GRATITUDE, BABY!

One of the best ways to keep perspective on what's important is to be grateful for what you've got. My blissfuls understood gratitude and the importance of expressing it with their partners, through thick and through thin.

In fact, many, many blissfuls stated that gratitude is what kept them happy, both with their partners and with their lives in general. Realizing the good things they had with their partners gave them a sense of appreciation, energy and lightness.

Gratitude is about both thanking your partner when he or she does something for you or on your behalf and just having a general sense of thankfulness in your life. For my blissfuls, it means never *not* thanking a partner when he or she does something for them ("Why *wouldn't* you say thanks?" one blissful asked incredulously). There's no reason not to...unless you're in a position where you don't respect your partner. In which case you've got other issues to resolve.

Like the path to bliss itself, gratitude is an ongoing thing. Showing it to your partner just once won't get you a happy relationship. It's part of the continual, nurturing process that leads to a strong, happy partnership...which adds to your overall bliss.

An entrepreneur in her 50s who has been married twice (as has her current husband) began her story with the role gratitude plays in their partnership:

> *"My husband has always been proud of me. Even when I took money out of my 401(k) for my business he told me to go for it...he said he'd work and hold us together for a while. He was and is so supportive. I'm thankful for that every day. I don't take him for granted ever. I thank him to this day for things like picking up the dry cleaning. I always tell him that I'm grateful. Nobody—not my husband or my kids—would ever say they don't know how much I love them or appreciate them. I always tell them I love them. It's a constant effort."*

She wraps up with this crucially important point...

> *"You just never stop trying to do better at this."*

Well said, my blissful. Well said.

ONE LAST BLISSFUL THOUGHT...

Before we get to the reflective questions I have one more quote, and it's from a blissful who has been happily married to his wife for decades. I include it because when I asked him the keys to his blissful partnership, he summed up so many of the points made in this chapter so beautifully, and in just a few sentences:

> *"All along we have allowed each other to find the work or fun we need in life without being too critical or demanding. We're okay having fun time that's separate from each other, allowing for a separate social life. But we also take time for each other, often going out twice during the week and then Saturday mornings. I will say that we have more time now that the kids are older. The most stressful time for us was when they were younger and we spent so much time driving them around. We tried to do a lot of the kids' stuff together, but we also divided and conquered sometimes. At that time we also allowed the other person to get away from the family stuff, too, and do their own things. The funny thing is we've never really discussed this stuff. We've just always known how to stay connected to each other."*

BLISS BUILDER EXERCISE
Your Blissful Life Partnership

Time to continue your reflections on your current level of bliss...and the journey to even more.

As with Chapter 4, the *Bliss Builder* exercise below is for general reflection. In this case the questions help you explore what your own blissful primary partnership might look like, and—if you're in one—what kind of bliss level you're at right now.

As you answer the questions below (on your own or at *www. bogusbalance.com*), please remember that this information is for you alone. No one is judging you or your answers (which means you're not allowed to judge yourself, either!).

1. What kind of primary partnership would you like to have? Describe it. What does it look like? How do you feel in it?

2. Now, specifically...

    a. What kind of support do you want?

    b. What level of intimacy?

    c. What kind of communication would work best for you? Describe it.

    d. Which of these are the highest priorities?

3. If you are currently in a primary relationship...

    a. How do you feel about it in general?

    b. How is this similar to or different from your intentions about your blissful partnership?

    c. How does this impact you and your life on a day-to-day basis?

    d. What does a day with your partner look like?

    e. Based on the tips from my blissfuls, what are some changes you might want to consider to get you closer to your definition of a blissful relationship?

    f. What is the best way to approach your partner to communicate these ideas?

4. Assessing your readiness for a blissful life partnership...

    a. How able are you to allow your partner to make decisions about his or her needs or goals, even if they differ from decisions you would make?

    b. How will you feel when your partner needs to engage in activities that have nothing to do with you?

    c. How will you feel when your partner achieves his or her own goals, even when they have nothing to do with you?

    d. What do you need to do to be the most blissful primary partner possible?

Now, keeping in mind your responses above and noting the themes, complete the following sentences:

In general, my blissful primary partnership will look like this:

In general, I believe taking the following steps will help me to achieve it:

Good work!

Now, we dig a little deeper into your primary relationships—the blissful family life you have or hope to have.

Again, if you need to take a little bit of time to decompress or reflect further on the work you've done already, by all means please do so. We will meet again soon in Chapter 6.

See you there...

BLISS BIT

"I would describe a blissful life as one that is filled with good health, good times, helping others and making the most of each day."

CHAPTER 6

The Blissful Family Life

"There's a day I'll die and I know my family will be there, holding my hand."

—BLISSFUL MAN IN HIS 50s

TALK ABOUT NEEDING to find balance...for real! What's become clear through my bliss-search is that the issue of parenting is *the* burning issue for people who are searching to feel sane, to feel even a little bit balanced. To them, the bogus balance concept—the one where you can have *it all* and do *it all* and be *it all* to everyone—is particularly challenging.

As we know, having *it all* isn't possible. But being truly balanced, having *your all,* and finding bliss in the process, is indeed possible. Having kids just makes it a bit trickier.

Now, before delving into the burning issue of parenting, let's get something out of the way.

I'm not a parent and I'm not going to be one. And so I am in no position to judge what the struggles of parenting must be like. I can surmise, of course. And I've seen it all around me.

I've seen the angst of parents rushing around as the workday comes to an end, breathlessly hoping they will get out on time and pick up their kids from their after-school programs before the penalty clock (and related fees) start ticking away.

I've seen parents arrive at a meeting or lunch with tears of either sadness or frustration after just having had an episode with a child who didn't want to be left behind...didn't want to cooperate with the day's plan...didn't want to get dressed... didn't want to wear the left shoe specifically, et cetera.

I've seen parents who just look so tired. I've heard many, many parents tell tales of sleepless nights, of the newfound ability to dig into places they never knew existed to find the energy to get through the day.

Of course, I've also heard lots of wonderful parenting stories...gleeful stories about the happiness parenting can bring to a life. And I'm sure these are just as true, and make all of the other tales, the ones about the struggle, worth it.

I'll also say that I heard from at least one person, a working mother of two, that having a family actually helps her find balance, helps her focus on what truly matters simply because her time is so limited. She said she is forced to make thoughtful choices about how she spends her day because she wants to ensure she can spend time with her kids and fulfill her parental obligations. She simply doesn't have the luxury of wasting time on things that don't matter.

It's a great point, though it doesn't take away from the fact that so many people have found parenting to be a tricky issue when it comes to both finding balance and finding bliss. And while I'm in no position to provide personal guidance on either when it comes to parenting, many of my blissfuls are. And they did. In fact, they were extremely eager to share the challenges faced and wisdom gained on this topic with me and with each other.

I'm happy that they did, because it seems the tough choices that need to be made by parents—and the guilt and the emotional toll that bringing up the lives of others can take—aren't talked about enough. For some reason, so much of what we read about parenting is how lovely and fulfilling and beautiful it is. And I know it is. But that doesn't mean that raising children isn't hard sometimes...it certainly doesn't make balancing life any easier.

Which is why we're talking about it here.

Behold, the collected themes, wisdom and tips from my blissfuls...

1. BE VERY, VERY INTENTIONAL ABOUT WHEN YOU HAVE YOUR CHILDREN.

This first tip is actually one that I *can* relate to, simply because of the constant barrage of questions I've received from people (during both my first and second marriages) about just when I was planning to have my first child. The pressure was on.

These inquiring individuals weren't trying to be inappropriate, of course. What this issue speaks to, however, is the assumption by many that the natural sequence of life includes school... then college...then marriage...then baby. While changing times means this sequence of events isn't quite so guaranteed, the question of "baby" is still very much a regular topic among lots of eager individuals.

When it comes from family members or friends who believe having children is simply the next natural step for you, the pressure and even the temptation to get started on expanding your own family as soon as possible can be great.

Visions of baby showers and baby-powder smells and baby visits to the park can be very powerful. These visions and their associated pressures can be so strong that whether or not to have a child (or wait to have one) isn't even a question. Many of my interviewees, especially the women, said that having children was just something they…did next. Many said they didn't so much plan to have them as much as *not* plan *not* to have them, leaving things up to chance once they got married.

My blissfuls had some specific advice on this. When it came down to the lessons learned, many said that the choice to have a child *in the first place* is a decision neither to be assumed nor taken lightly. And for the many, many people who do want to have children, the decision as to *when* to have them is one of the most important decisions people can make on their blissful journey.

Several women in my blissful focus groups said it is absolutely critical for those planning to have children to be honest with themselves about what parenting is and is not. They said individuals need to think about what it means to be a parent and what it will feel like—physically, mentally and emotionally.

Yes, it was pointed out by both my blissfuls and my other interviewees that it's actually impossible to truly know what being a parent will be like until it happens. But they all agreed that it's still important to paint as realistic a picture as possible when decisions are being made. This includes asking those who have experienced it (and whom you trust) to share the full picture on parenthood, speaking with financial and education professionals (whom you trust) about the kind of planning and resources you will need, and reading and viewing and listening to resources that will help you assess your own parenting readiness.

Readiness includes the readiness of you and your partner together, the readiness of you and your career and the readiness of you—physically, mentally and emotionally.

Based on this, some will make the intentional decision to have children early. Some will make the intentional decision to wait until they get to a certain place in their lives or careers. The important thing is to make an *intentional* decision—for you and the blissful life you intend to have.

2. KNOW THAT SACRIFICE IS PART OF IT.

Yes, there are a lot of positive aspects to having children, and neither I nor my blissfuls want to diminish this. At the same time, my blissfuls did share a common theme when talking about raising a family: sacrifice.

Sacrifice, of course, is about giving something up in order to get something else. It's not necessarily a bad thing, and my blissfuls didn't intend it to be so. But it is the reality. As we've discussed again and again, you just can't have *it all* and be blissful. Instead, you need to have *your all.* You must make choices, not just about what matters, but about what matters *most* to you, and go after it with intentionality and glee.

Nowhere did this idea come up more in my bliss-search than bringing up a family. Having children, and raising them well, means sacrificing other things. Period. It's critical to understand this point right from the start.

Parents talked often about sacrificing time with their friends in order to take care of their kids. They talked about sacrificing dream vacations in order to save money for future college tuitions. They talked about sacrificing a very close relationship with their kids in order to be more present at work. No matter which way it went, sacrifice was part of the game.

Knowing this, it's then up to you to decide what kind of parent you want to be, what your greatest values are in this regard, and what you will need to sacrifice in order to achieve your parenting goals. Once you decide this, once you commit to it, then resentment resulting from that sacrifice shouldn't be an issue. Or at least, not as often.

A retired executive in his 60s talked about how he went about being successful at his career, but also being the kind of father he knew he wanted to be:

"Carving out the right amount of time for family was a great challenge. I knew it was important to be a good dad and husband and so I just intrinsically knew I'd have to give things up to achieve it. So when buddies called up to play poker, I just said 'no.' I also knew that I'd sometimes have to give up sleep. When my kids were in college they'd be honored for various awards, and I'd get up at 4 a.m. to drive up and take them out to lunch to celebrate. Because I chose it, it actually never felt like sacrificing. It was a no-brainer. I have no regrets."

3. PRIORITIZE...TOGETHER.

Sound familiar? That's because you just read about this one in the last chapter about primary partnerships. And prioritizing together is never more important than when it comes to raising kids.

Once you've decided you want to have kids, and you know what you will sacrifice in order to do it the way you want to, you need to plan. And if you have a partner, you need to plan with him or her. For real.

As the blissfuls revealed in our last chapter, one of the tricky things about partnerships is that both people may have been brought up with very different experiences and values, which includes ideas about what it means to raise a family and what kinds of values you will want to integrate. It is a mistake to assume that simply because you and your partner agree on which kind of television to watch or how well-done you both like your beef, you will agree on how to raise a child.

Talk beforehand about what raising a family means to you, what you believe the various roles to be and how you want to go about it all. Know early where the gaps are so that you can work through them. Prioritize how the caregiving will go, and how various other priorities like careers and personal interests will be impacted (and, perhaps, sacrificed).

What's clear is that raising a child is wonderful, but also stressful and exhausting. My blissfuls were quite clear that it's a mistake to wait until you are knee-deep in it to figure these things out.

Remember that there are no right or wrong answers to this. Whether you choose to have one parent stay home, have both parents work full-time or come up with another solution is up to you and your partner. Just decide before you're in it.

A man in his 50s who is extremely ambitious and in absolute love with his career knew that he'd need to find a special kind of partner—one who could accept having a partner who made his career such a high priority. One who could accept and embrace how this would impact their family. (FYI: This might sound like the same man who was quoted in an earlier chapter, who spoke about hiking with both his wife and his cell phone. It's not.)

Here's how he and his wife went about raising their family:

> *"When we had our two kids (one year apart), both of us were working full-time. We both did our best to do our part, but when I took a promotion I knew it would impact my ability to give to the kids as much as I was before. My wife and I talked about it and she said she was comfortable taking on a bigger role with the kids. She's not as passionate about her job as I am about mine. Now she works two days each week, enough to keep her hand in her business while also taking on some of the heavier lifting at home. She really gets more enjoyment in taking care of the kids than working and it's just an understanding we have."*

Again, nothing is right or wrong here. In this person's case, it's about what he and his partner decided as a team before things got too messy. Plus, he knows he lucked out. He went on to say this…

> *"If not for being with the right person, I wouldn't still be married. She understands who I am. Not only that, she loves the enthusiasm I have for what I do and respects that."*

4. MANAGE THE GUILT.

Yep, there's that guilt monster again. Many of the people I interviewed (including virtually every respondent in the women's groups) said the guilt factor was *huge* in the specific area of kids. These individuals didn't just feel a little bit guilty a little of the time. The feeling was with them all the time, pertaining to both their kids and their work…and, it seems, everything else.

When they dropped their kids off or thought of them during the day, they felt like they weren't spending enough time with them. When they were with them or had to leave work early to take care of an issue, they felt like they were letting down their bosses. (To be clear, many men also felt the lingering emotion of guilt, though it wasn't communicated with the consistency of the women in my bliss-search.) And if guilt wasn't something the women were dealing with that very day, it was certainly something they'd dealt with in the past.

Even my blissful group was susceptible to the guilt monster, though they found ways to deal with their guilt so the monster was kept at bay most of the time (remember, even a blissful life isn't a perfect life).

Though I wish I could say that my blissfuls were able to offer a perfect solution to the guilt factor, unfortunately it's not that simple. Despite my repeated inquiries for ideas on how to get rid of guilt, there seemed to be no quick fix …nor was there a permanent solution for everyone.

Instead, it's clear that dealing with guilt—and keeping it from happening in the first place—takes an enormous amount of work with that persnickety mind of yours. It takes disciplined self-talk related to many of the concepts we've discussed thus far: deciding what's important and keeping perspective on your priorities over time, and intentionally choosing partners and careers and positions that allow you to embrace what will bring you bliss. And when things hit the fan—as they will—having a support system in place to help you deal with your guilt is key. There are some times when it doesn't get any better than validation from someone who's been there.

One of my blissfuls, a female employee in her 50s, talked about how this helped her deal with her guilt back when she was a single mom:

> "When my kids were babies and I was working, I kept feeling like I should have a better handle on everything. I had a friend who was also a single parent and put me at ease by saying that she also worked during those years, and she couldn't be prouder of her kids today. It made it all sound so achievable. It was so important for me to hear that. It relaxed me."

The guilt monster is very skilled at its craft. As we discussed in the chapter on how you make things more bogus for yourself, your brain can tell you all kinds of stories about what you're doing that might not be good enough. Much of it is unreal or an exaggerated and dramatic form of the truth. You need to know this. You need to tell yourself this. You need to make decisions that you know are true to you and stick with them, so that you will be confident that what you are doing is what you intended. When you make decisions about your priorities and what/who will make up your stew, and then go after it all authentically and intentionally, you will set yourself up for better bliss from the beginning.

A final word on guilt for now. One of the most important weapons against guilt has to do with our recent discussion about ego. It has to do with your own self-worth, with knowing you have made good choices and trusting yourself. When you trust yourself, when you know that you have chosen a life that brings bliss to you and those you choose to have around you, then the lens through which you choose to view your life and the pieces in it will be that much more positive, making it easier to work your way through your guilt when it pops up. When you know you are worthy just for being you, you won't feel like a bad person when you show up at work with baby spit-up on your shirt.

Remember, this journey is about being true to you. It's also about knowing who you are and not needing some "perfect parent" ribbon to tell you that you're a loving, valuable person taking care of other loving, valuable people.

5. GET YOUR SUPPORT TEAM IN PLACE, BUT...

As we talked about in the last tip, there's no doubt that the support team you have around you is critical (we'll cover this in greater depth in the next chapter).

But.

Just remember that your support team—and lots of other people—will also be eager to offer advice about how you can fix your situation, how you should go about parenting, how you should go about managing your career and how you should get your partner to take on his or her role.

While advice from those you trust can be very helpful, it's also important to remember that nobody truly knows your situation or your values the way you do. So keep this in mind as the people in your life tell you there's no other option but to quit your job or demand certain things from your boss or partner. Listen, ponder what works for you and graciously leave the rest behind you.

6. WHO'S THE BOSS?

It turns out that the boss, as we discussed in the chapter on the blissful career, matters a whole lot more than many of us think at first. And this includes how things go when you are working and raising a family at the same time.

If you are in a situation where you have a boss, make sure this person will support you in your child-raising values and plan. Of course, remember that you have signed up for a specific job and set of outcomes, and know that finding an understanding boss doesn't mean finding one who will let you off the hook from your responsibilities. Nor should it.

What it does mean is finding someone who appreciates that you want to have and raise a family, and will support you if you need to put family first in certain situations.

A few blissfuls pointed out that one factor in finding a supportive boss is to find one who is or was also involved in raising a family in some way. There's a difference between someone trying to understand what you're going through when trying to balance out your work and family responsibilities and someone who's doing it or has done it as well.

One blissful, an employee in her 50s, illustrated the point this way:

"The first seven years of my son's life were with me as the single parent. During that time I had a boss who had also been a single parent, and he both validated me and supported me. He told me I'd be fine, and also helped move me to new positions, ones with more flexibility."

Now, this being said, having a boss who is in a similar situation is just one consideration when choosing a boss while having a family…and it's certainly not a full-proof strategy. Nor is it a necessity.

The best thing to do is determine how you want to go about raising your family and communicate it to your boss early. Don't wait until you have to rush home from work because your baby has a fever to find out that your boss thinks this is unacceptable. It's really not fair to either of you.

If you find that your current job or boss is not conducive to your raising a family the way you want to or in a way that matches your values, then you need to sit down and make your choice (there's that word again) about how you want to handle it. And determine if you need to make a change in some way.

One of my blissfuls talked about raising her child years ago, while working at a bank. She said her "aha!" moment came when she arrived home from work and her baby daughter said to her, "Hi, Dad." She was crushed when she realized her daughter didn't know her well enough to distinguish her from others. It was unacceptable to her.

So she changed it. She quit her job and took another position that paid less but allowed her to be more flexible. She also changed her mindset, and realized that she didn't need to go above and beyond the call of duty at the office *every single time* as she'd been doing. She realized that she could be productive and appreciated at work simply by doing her job well.

Another working mom, now in her 50s, talked about making

a change once she realized that the hardest part of parenting was all of the unexpected things that came up—the last-minute news that she had been "signed up" to bring cupcakes to the classroom that day, or when one of her daughters informed her late in the day that she needed a ride to a school event. She also said that part of the difficulty and guilt came from just not being there with her children enough, and from knowing they were waiting for her at home while she was finishing up work. Here's more from her:

> *"There's this need from your kids for your presence. You get home and then your kids want your attention, and your husband does, too. Eventually I realized I needed to change the way I went about my job. I started working from home and found it made all the difference in being there for my family as well as my career."*

Her choice not only helped her find balance, but helped her feel like she was being true to herself, which helped her feel blissful. She could honor her highest priorities—her career and her family life—knowing that even though these parts of her stew might overlap, she was doing what she wanted with both in a way that fit her. Yes, she had to give up time at the office with her colleagues, which was a sacrifice to her, but to her this was worth it.

The added benefit for this blissful was that she realized how much she actually liked working from home. Today, even though her daughters are now grown, she continues to work from home and says she'll never go back to work in an office setting.

7. SELF-WHAT?

The issue of self-care is coming up in Chapter 8, so I'm not going to dive too deeply into it here...*except* to say that there is no more important nor tricky time to engage in self-care than when you have kids.

It's important because...well...you have kids. And you want to be at your best when you are spending time with them, caring for them and disciplining them.

It's tricky because...well...you have kids. Which means your time can feel limited, like it's been swallowed up whole by all of the parental duties and activities you have on your plate.

My blissful parents understand this challenge. They also say it must be overcome. If you don't take proper care of yourself, if you don't give yourself the time to relax, recharge and engage in activities that fulfill you, then you simply won't have the energy and stamina you need to be the best blissful parent you can be.

At a loss about how to do this exactly? Stay tuned.

8. KNOW YOUR KIDS WILL BOUNCE. MOST OF THE TIME.

I'll never forget the first time I heard this phrase. It came from a co-worker who brought her young daughter into the office for a few hours.

I was sitting at the reception desk and watching her toddler toddle about, exploring every corner of the space, teetering up stools and boxes that led her to the higher shelves.

I immediately got nervous as she aimed higher and higher, and told my colleague that her daughter was climbing around. Her response? "She'll be okay. Kids bounce."

At first I was taken aback by what seemed like some pretty

casual parenting. And while I'm not saying it's a healthy parenting technique to let your child climb all over the place without paying attention, I do think her grander point makes sense. I can only imagine how hard it is to keep an eye on a child every second, and how trying to eliminate every single point of risk could be unnecessary, exhausting and—in the end—not a good thing for the kids themselves.

Her point was that children are more resilient than we give them credit for being. And they can bounce back from a lot.

I heard this concept again from one of my blissfuls who had raised her kids as a single working mom for several years. Over time she realized she didn't have to be with her kids every second, taking care of their every need, to be a good parent. In fact, she realized that giving them their own space would actually benefit them later on.

Here's how she put it:

> *"The main lesson I learned from that time was that you can expect a lot from your kids. It's better for them to be full participants in how things work, and they respect you for not being a slave to them. My kids weren't exactly* feral *[she said with a laugh], but there were other parents who thought they were. No matter. My kids knew enough that they could do things like start dinner or schedule their own carpool. It wasn't easy, but it worked fine and my kids are normal."*

ONE LAST BLISSFUL THOUGHT...

Another lovely summary of blissful parenting tips came from a mom in her 40s, one who stayed at home to raise her kids when they were younger. This blissful made it clear that she very much enjoyed her role as a stay-at-home mom. What she also made clear is how critical it was to find strategies to help parents ensure that they are getting as much bliss out of raising their kids—and out of life in general—as possible. So she did.

Here's what she said:

> *"Back when I was a new mom, there were certain aspects of being with babies all the time that were frustrating. I found myself getting obsessed and focusing on them all of the time, worrying if they weren't sleeping well, worrying about them getting sick. It can take over your mind. I joined play groups and found others in similar situations. I forced myself to have something to look forward to every day. I also knew I had a partner who would come home and I looked forward to our adult conversation. Over time I also realized that the things that frustrated me pertaining to the kids would always pass. Things change so quickly with children. It's all like a phase."*

BLISS BUILDER EXERCISE
Your Blissful Family Life

Ready to keep on going? Your journey continues with your next set of *Bliss Builder* questions, which will get you reflecting on your own blissful family life. Take some time to answer the questions below (on your own or at *www.bogusbalance.com*). Remember, no judgy-judgy—nobody's watching. And even if they were, it's not their business.

1. If you do not currently have kids...

   a. What does your blissful family life of the future look like? How does it feel? Describe it.

b. What do you need to figure out, work on or get into place (with you and/or with your partner) before you feel ready to start a family?

2. If you currently have one or more children...

a. What kind of blissful family life would you like to have? What does it look like? How does it feel? Describe it.

b. Describe your current family life. How is it similar to or different from your vision of a blissful family life? What is working best? What isn't working at all?

c. In your blissful vision, how much time are you spending on the family part of your life stew?

d. How much time are you actually spending on the family part of your life stew?

e. What about your primary partnership (if you're in one) is working toward your blissful family life?

f. What changes in your primary partnership (if you're in one) would help create a more blissful family life?

g. How can you go about communicating your ideas above with your partner in an effective way?

h. How much alone time do you need in order to be your best with your blissful family?

i. Based on the tips from my blissfuls, what are some other changes you might want to consider to get you closer to a blissful family life?

Now, keeping in mind your responses above and noting the themes, complete the following sentences:

In general, my blissful family life will look like this:

In general, I believe taking the following steps will help me to achieve it:

Bravo, my friend. Bravo!

Ready to move on to our next topic? It's a good one. In fact, I think you'll really like it.

As usual, take a break for reflection and maybe a nap or a snack (or both).

And when you're ready…onward!

BLISS BIT

"There's a certain element of bliss that comes simply with being content with what you have in that moment."

CHAPTER 7

The Blissful Others

"He and I are both CEOs, so we get each other.
We can vent to each other."

—BLISSFUL MAN IN HIS 60s

THIS ONE IS important. It's so important, in fact, that I've found different ways to bring it up in my last two books...and yet still feel the need to bring it up again here. As its own chapter.

Here's why.

One of the most important things you can do to find and retain your bliss is to gather the right people around you—your blissful others. These blissful others, the ones you choose to have in your life, play two critical roles on your journey.

First of all, they're just fun, blissful people to have in your life. They share in your blissful experiences, even experiencing the bliss right along with you. They come up with interesting, stimulating, fun ways to spend the day. They smile and it's infectious. They are positive, filled with whatever kind of energy you need to supplement your personality. They shine a light on your life. And you shine a light on theirs.

The second role these "right" people play in your life is as a sturdy support mechanism. They aren't just a part of some of your blissful experiences; they also provide the underlying support you need to achieve your bliss when things aren't quite as blissful as you want them to be.

Let's face it. There will be moments when your confidence or efforts related to this blissful journey will slip. It's natural and it happens to us all. After all, chances are your blissful journey requires some change and more than a little uncertainty, and both of these can feel pretty scary (more on this to come). At some point it may make perfect sense to veer directly off your blissful journey, to retreat back to where you came from...not because it makes you feel balanced, and certainly not because it makes you happy, but because you know it, you're accustomed to it and there's no risk.

Now we both know that when this happens, you must find a way to keep on going. You have decided you want and deserve a blissful life, and so a blissful life you shall have.

When the fear comes, you will need some blissful others in your life to keep you on track. You will need people around you to remind you of your blissful goals, and to remind you that you deserve them. You will need people to call on when you begin to feel guilty, when you begin to feel selfish for putting yourself first (you're *not* selfish, by the way).

You need people who will validate you, tell you that they understand that this is hard, kindly give it to you straight when you're making excuses or telling yourself bogus stories and hold your proverbial hand during the journey whenever you need it. Perhaps every step of the way.

My blissfuls knew this. And, as always, they had some thoughts to share on the whole issue of your blissful others. Let's get to them...

1. JUST WHO ARE THESE BLISSFUL OTHERS...AND WHO *AREN'T* THEY?

Let's get a bit more specific about these blissfuls others.

Just what will they be like, exactly?

These people will be positive. They will be hopeful. And they will be believers in *you*. They will tell you how amazing you are for being on this journey in the first place.

Sure, they will let you whine when you need to whine, but they'll let you know when you've exhausted your whining privileges. They will give you a few minutes in the pity pot, but they won't jump in there with you for the day. They will not be about commiserating with you unless it's to validate you. They will cheer you on enthusiastically and will feel only delight when you achieve new heights.

You will feel comfortable around these blissful others. You will know that they are acting and speaking in the ways they do because they truly care about you. You will not feel judged. You will not feel afraid to share parts of your journey. You will trust these people. And they will honor you.

And you will do the same for them. Because they are your right fit. They are your awesome others.

Though it's not mandatory of course, some of your blissful others may be those who are in similar situations as you. Perhaps they've got a similar professional/personal mix and can relate to your struggles. Perhaps they are also engaging in change and all that comes with it. Perhaps there is something you can teach each other. Sometimes all you need to know in order to feel better about the whole deal is that you're not the only one going through a challenge.

Here's an example, and it's related to our last chapter. A stay-at-home mom in her 40s discussed the importance of her blissful others team, especially when she was new at her mom role:

"By finding and creating a network of other new moms who were in the same boat as me, I never felt alone or depressed or resentful about that stage of life. It was so helpful. Even though I was peed on, pooped on, spit up on (sometimes all in the same day)…and some days exhausted…I still felt lucky and blessed to be living life the way my husband and I wanted to."

Now, if the relationships I described above feel too good to be true, I assure you that they're not. What this means is that the support system you currently have in your life is not filled with the people you need to stand closely with you as you walk this journey.

And that's okay. The most important thing is to get your blissful others in place now, which means knowing both who *is* and who *is not* a blissful other.

And who, exactly, are your *who-is-nots*? The judgers, the critics, the creators of doubt.

With your blissful others there will be no competition. No gossip-mongering. No misery-loving-some-company here.

You must be sure not to weaken and let in your *who-is-nots*…even if you've known them for a lifetime. Even if their negativity brings comfort in a way. That negativity can create a serious barrier on your journey. And that's not what you want. It's not. Even if you don't cut your *who-is-nots* out completely (sometimes it's not possible), be careful with what you tell them and how you involve them in your life.

Now, what do you do if you don't have any or enough blissful others in your life at the moment? Well then, it's time to find them! This means taking the time to notice who around you— at work, at your gym, at your parenting group, in your social circles—makes you smile, who clicks with you, who gives off good, positive energy. It might also mean exposing yourself to new groups of people. Volunteering for a cause you care about or joining a social group that focuses on your interests are great strategies. They allow you to meet new people so that you can scope out who has "blissful other potential," while at the same time engaging in an activity that matters to you.

Another note before we move on.

It's important to know that just because you've decided to begin this journey to bliss and make change doesn't mean others are aware of it, that they're in a place where they can support you in what you need or that they will want to be a part of it at all.

Be careful about your expectations when selecting your blissful others, and even when you're just engaging with those around you who have been a part of your life for a while. Do not expect someone who has never shown you support to now offer it just because you are in this new place. Do not expect a dysfunctional pattern that has formed over years to simply change in a week because you've set a boundary. Acknowledge the relationships and dynamics that exist, make your plan on who you will and will not invite on this journey and be realistic. There's no reason to create frustration for you and others because you want others to change now that you are changing.

In the end, the people you find yourself identifying as your blissful others might surprise you. It might just be that your best friend since junior high can no longer give you what you need for this part of your journey. And it might be that the person you met just one month ago in the break room at work provides the perfect energy.

Some of the people you recruit into your team of blissful others may change. Some may go. Some new people may be added. That's okay. It's better to be intentional about your choices throughout the process, and your needs may change. Because even though, in the end, how and when you achieve your bliss is up to you, the actions or words of even one person can cause significant help or harm along the way.

2. YOUR BLISSFUL ACCOUNTABILITY COPS.

There is another, quite helpful role that some of your blissful others will offer you: accountability cop. These are the people who will help you stick to your journey…the ones who will check in with you, who will ask you how you are feeling, who will see if you've taken certain steps you have committed to on your path. Who will strongly but gently help you get back on track when needed.

Intentionally think through who might play this role. You will also need to decide just how that person will hold you accountable to your journey and your commitments. Is it someone who checks in each week and asks a specific question about a step you planned to take? Is it someone you see for lunch once or twice each month just to talk through your latest progress? Is it someone who offers to be on "blissful call" for you so that you can reach out to him or her the moment any doubts, fears or guilt come into play?

Truly think through how such people will help you stick to your path and let them know you need them to play this role… and that it's an important one. It's amazing what happens when you know someone is going to hold you accountable. You'll find yourself taking the steps you need to take, if for no other reason than to avoid having to admit otherwise or disappoint the person. Funny how our minds work, yes?

And when your accountability cops perform their duty, appreciate it and do your best not to get frustrated. After all, you asked them to do it. It's not their fault when they remind you of your commitment to yourself and your blissful life…and hold you to task on finding happiness.

A retired media executive in his 70s looked back on his time as an intense, driven CEO and knew that listening to his blissful others was especially important to help him stay introspective. Here's his advice:

"It's very important to take a step back and to listen to the key people around you...your kids, your wife, your best friends. Let's face it, when you're a driven person you don't listen too well. So at least focus on hearing the words of those you respect."

3. THE STICKY FAMILY DYNAMIC.

We all know that we don't choose our families. While some beloved family members can give you exactly what you need to find bliss, others can't. In fact, they may actually create barriers and challenges all along the way.

No matter how they help or hurt your journey, families—unlike most of the others in your life—are here to stay. Those whose family members create more hindrance than help face a difficult challenge, to be sure. Unless they choose to take drastic measures and cut their families out of their lives completely (which I'm not recommending, but which is a decision made by some), there may be some hindering family presence involved.

The thing to consider is how to have less dysfunction over time. Who might be seen less? With whom might you set boundaries? Whom might you just need to steer clear of for the time being? And who in the family might understand you enough to help you with this? If the answer is nobody, then it's good to know that now, and act accordingly by finding others who will support you and leaving family members out of it. Your family will see in time that you are happier, but they don't necessarily need to know all the steps you are taking along the way.

Know that your decisions about your family won't necessarily be understood. A sister who brings a whole lot of negative energy may feel pretty hurt if you decrease the time spent with her, for instance. It's important in these cases to be sensitive and kind, but to also hold true to who you really are and what you want. The guilt monster might rise up big time in this process, but you can be strong. You can take the stand and set the boundaries you need to help you on your journey.

After all, if you don't do this, nobody else will do it for you.

A FEW WORDS OF WARNING...

Before moving on from this topic of your blissful others, there's one more important point to cover.

Yes, you want to rely on the support of others. You want to hear their advice, sometimes seek out their counsel.

But.

As I mentioned in the last chapter, this is *your* journey. This is *your* bliss. Lots of people will have lots of advice on how you should proceed. But they are not you, and their journey is different.

The one person who can ensure you are on the right path to your bliss is you. You know yourself best and you are your own advocate.

So choose your team of blissful others well, ask them for support when you need it, and always remember that whether or not you live a blissful life comes down to the choices you yourself make in it.

Sometimes you'll just need a little bit of help to get there.

And, if you choose right, your blissful others will make sure you do.

BLISS BUILDER EXERCISE
Your Blissful Others

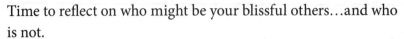

Time to reflect on who might be your blissful others...and who is not.

Give the *Bliss Builder* exercise below some time and let your authentic answers come as you respond (on your own or at *www.bogusbalance.com*). Know that this just a first step in determining your team. You will have a better sense of who you want around you as you continue through the book and complete your blissful plan in Chapter 9.

This set of questions might feel particularly tricky, especially when you get to the part where you name names. But remember, nobody's watching. And this is too important to rush through without being true to yourself. You might find there are duplicate answers, or that names pop up more than once. That's okay. In fact, it will probably tell you some things.

1. Describe the blissful others you will need with you on this journey. What are their characteristics? How do they communicate? What kind of support do they offer?

2. Who in your life matches this description? Who gives you positive energy? Who do you trust completely?

3. Who have you seen and felt energized by in the last three months?

4. Who do you feel might be a good accountability cop for you?

5. Who in your life takes away your energy? Who do you find focuses on the negative and/or drains you?

6. In the last three months, who have you allowed yourself to gossip with, complain with, be negative with?

7. Whose name makes you cringe when it comes across your cell phone, email inbox or other digital communication device?

8. Who will decidedly not be a blissful other on your journey? Are any of them family members?

9. How will you go about keeping the boundaries you need with each of them so that you can continue your journey the way you feel is necessary?

Now, keeping in mind your responses above and noting the themes, complete the following sentences:

I will include the following individuals among my blissful others on this journey:

I will include the following individuals as accountability cops:

I will not include the following individuals as blissful others on this journey:

Well done. Like I said, this one is tricky. I'm proud of you for doing it anyway.

Okay…it's now time to take those fingers that have been pointing to the blissful others and turn them around so that they're pointing straight at you. It's time to figure out how *you* will make a blissful you.

Take a breath, take a minute if you need to, and let's get down to it.

On to Chapter 8…

BLISS BIT

"Bliss is that moment, or span of time, when my world seems well-balanced, resolved, and I'm experiencing peace of mind. During this time my capacity for love (both expressed and received) is relatively higher. Some specific events or activities that are likely to trigger bliss include singing, sex, time working on projects that promise rewarding outcomes, a night out with people I love, a quiet moment with a cup of coffee, and a book on a day of no scheduled obligations."

CHAPTER 8

The Blissful You

"I am who I am."

—BLISSFUL MAN IN HIS 60s

WE'VE SPENT A lot of time thus far reflecting on various components of your blissful journey, and what you're going to need from others to help you achieve your bliss.

It's now time to focus on the most important person on this journey: you.

There are a few *you* components to this discussion, and we begin with a giant one. It can be a bit tricky to tackle, but it's crucial to your bliss. Here it is.

1. GET SQUARE WITH YOU.

I alluded to this back in the chapter on your blissful career, when we discussed how my blissfuls felt about their titles. Their titles were important to them, but they didn't define them. They didn't reflect their own worth in this world. My blissfuls already knew they were worthy, and so they didn't need something on the outside to tell them this.

They were square with themselves.

Getting square with you means knowing deep down that you are a capable person, that you are a smart person, that you are a valuable person...no matter what your title or your salary or the number of trophies your kids might win.

Sure, you will have goals, and they will be important...and they will mean something. They will illustrate some things you can do. But they won't define *who you are*. They won't define your value on this earth. And so your goals and your actions will be tied to what you love and enjoy most...not what will get you the fanciest title.

Being square with you means that you know that your worth is a strong, immovable high bar on the graph of your life, even if the ups and downs of your day-to-day climb and dip in all kinds of ways...reflecting achievements, disappointments, victories and mistakes.

It means making choices with confidence—not because you need to prove anything, but because you want to be true to yourself and be happy.

One of my blissfuls, an entrepreneur in her 50s, said being square with herself meant knowing she could do whatever she set her mind to do:

> *"For me it's about setting a goal and realizing that it's possible. It begins with belief...belief in yourself...belief that you can achieve it."*

In theory we'd all like to have this confidence in ourselves. We'd all like to be square with ourselves. But, it turns out, getting there isn't as easy as it sounds.

What *is* easy is getting swept up in the chatter all around us...the talk about how money equals greatness, the priorities placed on succeeding at all costs, the media stories glorifying those who reach the highest of heights in their work. When we succeed, we are told we are good. When we fail, we are told we are bad...or we are told nothing at all.

For many of us, these lessons first came when we were young. And we continue to have them reinforced today just by looking around us and listening to the hype.

These lessons can easily guide us in the wrong direction, encouraging us to make decisions in our lives based on getting that better title, that bigger salary, at all costs...because it will mean we're worth something.

But here's the thing. We're worth something *anyway*.

Stay with me. Because even if you think this issue doesn't apply to you, even if you pride yourself on your self-confidence, even if you can list your accomplishments on a long, long sheet of paper, you might be in this boat with the rest of us. In fact, if you feel the need to tell me how square you are with you, you might not be that square.

People who are square with who they are don't need to talk about their accomplishments, their titles, the achievements they've made. Not all the time, anyway.

Yes, to some extent it's perfectly fine to do so. Celebrating success is a lovely way to honor yourself.

But.

The problem comes when we tell others about our successes, titles, salaries and compliments not just to honor ourselves, but because we believe it will impress them. We believe they will respect us more. We believe they will accept us more, include us more, connect with us more. We believe they will have the opinion that we are not just good at what we *do*, but that we are good as a *person*. That we are better than we were before...perhaps better than others. And once we've convinced them that we're more worthy, we then get to believe it as well.

When this happens it's because we're not square with

ourselves. We need to hear validation from the outside because we're not getting what we need on the inside.

If you are not square with you, you don't believe that you are worthy and likeable and valuable *no matter what* your job, no matter what your salary, no matter what your accomplishments in life. And when titles and money and accomplishments matter so much that they actually define who you are, efforts to achieve them will eclipse everything else. They become the absolute top priority, over happiness and family and self-care and fun activities, because they become a part of your identity. They determine your worth as a person.

This totally messes with your blissful stew. It warps the process of decision-making about how you spend your time and how you prioritize, because there is so much at stake when it comes to your success, title and salary.

To be clear, there will certainly be times when less blissful choices need to be made due to commitments to your work, your goals and your craft. But these choices won't need to be made at *every* turn, in *every* moment. Some moments—lots of them, in fact—need to be about your happiness, the happiness of your loved ones, your personal health.

It's easy…and natural…to let our egos take over, to take pride in telling our colleagues about the big promotion and fancy new title. It's normal to want the approval and kudos of others.

But it's when we *need* that approval from them because we don't approve of ourselves that things get more complicated, and so do our choices. That's the difference.

Think about it for a minute…

- Do you have a great job title and tell everyone about it?

- Do you get to take great trips and love to tell everyone where you're going on your next adventure?

- Do you love to talk about the compliment you received during your last performance evaluation? Or the way you made everyone laugh at your business lunch?

I'll be the first to admit that I sure do. But I work to be aware of when I'm doing it *a lot*. I try to understand why I need to convince others that I'm worthy or valuable or loveable. I realize how my own self-worth (or lack thereof) might just be playing a part, and how the decisions I make as a result are impacting my happiness and health.

Here's a little checklist to drive home my point.

When you are square with you:

- you are aware of your values, needs and goals at any given moment, and will make decisions based on them even if others might not approve.

- you hear the opinions and feedback from others with interest, but also consult your own desires, wisdom and gut before making decisions.

- you don't constantly correct people when they get your title wrong. And you're not that impressed by the titles of others because you know we're all worthy in our own ways.

- you celebrate your successes with grace, and learn from your mistakes without shame. Your successes and failures will be results of things you've done, but not a determination of who you are.

- you know that you do great work, but that you are not irreplaceable...because none of us are. And you are fine with that.

- you give others credit and you apologize when you make mistakes. Sometimes you even apologize when you don't believe you've done anything wrong because you know it matters to someone else more than it does to you.

- you do not feel the need to make your part of your conversations with people (in person or on social media) all about the important things you've done.

- you are happier because of the choices you make. You are happier because you like yourself. You wear that happiness more, and it energizes those around you.

This issue of not being square with ourselves came up throughout my bliss-search. My non-blissfuls struggled with it regularly, and many of my current blissfuls shared stories of their low self-esteem from the past. They said they felt they had something to prove, not just as professionals, but as *people*. They felt the need to prove they weren't just good at their jobs, but so pristine that their bosses would never regret hiring them in the first place. Entrepreneurs felt they needed to be perfect at all times, with every client, in order to ever book a gig again.

Many of those struggling with this issue felt they needed to prove to *themselves* that they were actually good enough to be doing what they were doing. Those in a more traditional work setting needed to shake that feeling that they'd somehow duped their bosses into hiring them before they were good enough. Business owners needed to prove to themselves that they didn't blow it by starting a venture they weren't ready for. And somehow, that finish line of proof, that moment when they would actually believe they were good enough themselves, was never crossed. With every step of progress, the finish line kept moving forward as well.

One of my blissfuls, an organizational CEO in his 60s, said that his younger self always felt the need to prove his abilities to those around him. After stepping into a new and intense leadership position, he decided the hiring process wasn't enough to prove to others (and himself) that he was ready, so he decided to pursue his master's degree at the same time. He talks about the price he paid:

> "I actually told my partner at the time that I couldn't make him a priority. I told him that I had only one set of priorities, and that was my professional growth. Eventually, we broke up."

It was after the split that he realized he'd taken on a goal that wasn't just important to him, but that *defined* him. Today he's made changes for a happier, fulfilled, blissful life.

Okay, Deirdre, I get it, you might be thinking...*so just how can I get square with me?*

I will not pretend to have any kind of counseling, psychology, therapy or other degree relating to improving one's self-esteem. But I will say that a good first step is getting real with yourself, reflecting on whether or not you truly value and like yourself *no matter what.* If you don't, then the next step is to accept this without judgment. After all, most of us struggle with this. And even if we're generally square with ourselves, there are certainly times that we slip. Perhaps regularly.

Chances are if you're not square with you right now, if you think you need a grand title or salary or outside validation to matter, this is not a new thing. You might have learned it a long time ago...maybe believed it over a lifetime.

Once you recognize and accept this as an issue, then you can start doing something about it. You can speak with those you trust who might be dealing with it, too. You can do research on self-confidence and self-esteem, take a look at the (credible) books, videos and other resources that address this as an issue. You can explore the idea of affirmations, mantras or other tools that will work for you. If it feels right, you may want to consider improving your own sense of self-worth by working with a counseling professional.

That's what I did. It wasn't easy. It was messy. And I can still slip. But now I'm aware when it happens. I have the tools to get square again. Most of the time.

The important thing to know is that you are worthy no matter what. We all are. And you've got to believe this because you need to be your biggest advocate, your biggest supporter, your biggest believer. *That's* how you make decisions that truly balance you. *That's* how you make decisions that make you happy. That make you peaceful. That have meaning. That's how you find bliss.

Having others around you to remind you how good you are is wonderful, but it means nothing if you need it constantly because you don't believe it yourself. So believe it…or take steps to get there.

2. ENGAGE IN SELF-CARE. FOR EVERYONE'S SAKE.

Self-care is another one of those sticky issues that came up over and over in my bliss-search.

Self-care means, of course, taking care of yourself. It means knowing what you need physically, mentally and emotionally to be the best, most blissful you.

Bring up self-care and lots of people automatically think of images related to yoga, a golf game or a spa day. And maybe that will work for you. But self-care is really anything that will help you relax, recharge and re-center. It can be physical, mental or spiritual. It can include stimulating activities like taking a class or writing a blog. It can include relaxing activities like going for a quiet walk or getting a massage. It can include fun activities like spending time out with friends or attending a small musical concert. It can be done with people or done alone. It can be as simple as taking a few seconds for three deep breaths or getting an extra hour of sleep.

There are a few keys to self-care. The first is knowing what will be the most beneficial to you, what will help you relax, recharge and re-center.

The second key is to then actually *do* those things.

And this is where many people get stuck.

Why? Because of the time factor. Because of the guilt factor. Because there is so much to do and so much to manage and we get overwhelmed. Because we want to be needed and successful and reliable, and we don't want to mess that up by taking time to focus on ourselves.

Somehow, when we're in the midst of our lives, self-care turns into the notion that we are *selfish*. Which is completely bogus.

And so we negotiate. We put off the things that would qualify as self-care until everything else is done. And, over time, we decide that there's *never* a time that everything else is done. And so the self-care never happens.

Many non-blissful interviewees said that engaging in self-care just contributed to their guilt and stress, that they would spend the time thinking about all of the things and people and obligations awaiting them when it was over, and so they couldn't enjoy it.

My blissfuls, however, said to get over it. They knew that self-care didn't just contribute to their bliss, but also made them better at what they did overall.

One blissful said it's all about her physical activity:

> *"I've determined that taking time to exercise for one hour equals three hours of better productivity later."*

Another said simply:

> "Getting sleep is definitely an important part of the blissful equation."

Self-care doesn't just help you feel and work better, it also gives you a bit of space away from the things that you are so deeply enmeshed in all day long. It battles burnout. It reminds you that you—you *alone*—are worth spending time on (which helps you get square with you). It creates perspective, which is critical in finding new ways to go about your goals. It makes you happier, which makes you more fun to be around. It fills you, so that you can fully give of yourself to the rest of your stew. After all, if you're depleted, if you're empty, there's really nothing left to give to others, right?

Many of us know this in our heads, but make a whole lot of excuses as to why we can't engage in self-care when the time actually comes.

If this is you, stop. Build in time for the best self-care activities that will make you the person you want to be. It doesn't have to be a lot of time, but it needs to be there. Don't go more than a day or two without doing *something* that recharges you.

Brainstorm ideas that will be purely fun, that will feed you and give you new energy for the other parts of your stew. Think beforehand about what you will say or do to keep yourself on your self-care track when you are tempted to avoid it. Think about what you would say to friends if they gave you a bunch of bogus excuses as to why they couldn't take care of themselves properly. Ask others (people you trust) to hold you accountable if that helps.

Don't believe it helps? Test out the theory and see for yourself. Engage in self-care—*real* self-care with no guilt—for two weeks and see how you feel and live as a result. You can thank me later.

BLISS BUILDER EXERCISE
Your Blissful You

Ready to be the most blissful you that you can be? The *Bliss Builder* exercise below will help get you there, so respond with care (on your own or at *www.bogusbalance.com*).

The list begins with questions that will help determine whether you are truly square with you. For these questions especially, it's extremely important to be open and to avoid any temptations to justify yourself. Most of us deal with not being square with ourselves at one time or another. Just take a breath and plunge ahead.

1. Getting square with you...

   a. In general, how square do you believe you are with yourself?

   b. How often do you tell others about your accomplishments or the accomplishments of your children (whether in person, by email or through social media)? What do these accomplishments mean to you?

   c. How do you feel when you receive criticism from others? How do you respond?

   d. How do you let your daily successes impact you? Do you celebrate them? Do they define you as a person?

   e. How do you let your daily mistakes, errors or failures impact you? How do you handle them? Do they define you as a person? How long does it usually take for you to move on from them?

   f. Think about the last three days and the decisions you've made about your time, your activities and your engagement with others. How many of your decisions have been based on the need to prove yourself to others? To yourself?

g. How do you feel about yourself right now?

h. Do you believe you would still be worthy as a person if you got fired tomorrow? What if your partner left you or your child failed out of school?

i. What are some ideas you have to help you get more square with you? Where might you begin?

2. Getting your self-care in order...

a. What kinds of self-care activities would make you more blissful?

b. Which of these energize you the most?

c. What are some ways you can make the time to fit these into your life?

d. What is one self-care activity that you will do within the next 24 hours?

e. How will you feel when you do it? How will it also benefit others?

f. What are some ways you can hold yourself accountable to your self-care commitments?

Now, keeping in mind your responses above and noting the themes, complete the following sentences:

I believe the issue of self-worth is impacting my life in the following ways:

I commit to getting more square with myself, and I will take the following steps to do so:

> I commit to engaging in the following self-care activities, beginning immediately:

Whew…you've gotten so far!

Ready to get specific? Ready to figure out your passion and plan your specific path to bliss?

If you've chosen to skip taking a breather up to now, this is actually a good time to take a few moments and gather some extra-special energy. Because things are about to get even more blissful. And you want to be ready when it happens.

So get ready…your blissful blueprint awaits!

BLISS BIT

"I don't think of it as bliss, but as joy, which I find every day in different things. I feel relaxed, tranquil and happy. Sometimes I feel deep emotions. I love people, and get a high and joy from being around them. They make my heart sing."

CHAPTER 9

Your Blissful Plan

"Always keep the main thing the main thing."
—BLISSFUL MAN IN HIS 60s

WELL, HERE WE ARE. We're at an exciting, critical juncture. Before we continue, let's do a quick check-in, you and me.

Doing okay? I know you've reflected on a number of blissful components in your life, and that can feel overwhelming. My hope is that it's also feeling...well...hopeful.

After all, you are on your way to bliss. You have begun a journey that will make you happier. That, as a result, will make those around you happier, too. That will make you more successful, more connected to yourself. More connected to others.

You are making choices that will make you feel truly balanced, truly sane, truly happy. You are making choices that will get you to your bliss. You are doing this for yourself. And it is a tremendous thing you are doing. It is not selfish; it is not greedy. It doesn't mean you care about anybody else any less.

It just means that you care enough about yourself, and this life you're living, to make that life as blissful as it can be.

So now that you've done some good, healthy reflecting, it's time to get down to it.

It's time to figure out just what will make you blissful. For real.

It's time to figure out just what professional and personal components will be a part of your life stew, and the size each piece will take up in our little, edible metaphor.

It's time to figure out *your all.*

It's time to make choices, which means being *choosy.* It means being discerning, choosing certain things to focus on in your life *instead of* other things.

A few people have the luxury of knowing what they want in life since its beginning. (I interviewed one of them, that TV executive. Lucky guy.) The rest of us have to work at it. And then, after a while, we have to work at it again because, for many of us, what we want in life changes.

Figuring this out can feel heavy, as though it's a chore. But I encourage you to think about it differently. This work is not meant to be...work. It's meant to inspire. It's meant to excite. It's meant to be fun. It's meant to be blissful.

So use this time to play a bit. To dream of what your blissful life will look like.

Thinking of it this way isn't always easy, especially if you don't really know what you want or what you're *meant* to do. It can feel overwhelming, like one more hard thing to figure out.

That's why this is being done in a safe way. Right here.

After all, how can you reach bliss when you don't know what makes you blis*ful*? How can you know how to prioritize the pieces in your stew when you have no idea what those pieces are?

So let's figure out the pieces, yes?

PART I: FIGURING OUT YOUR BLISS

You begin to figure out your bliss by figuring out your passion.

I know. That word.

I actually hesitated to use it because the word *passion* is just so...*overused* these days. It feels squishy, touchy-feely, more than a bit clichéd.

But I'm using it anyway because it's relevant, and because I think you know what I mean by it. And because I think you know why it's important.

Think about it. You've got 24 hours a day to spend doing *something*. And you want to be blissful while you're doing it (I know this because you're reading this book). And you have choices in this to make sure that you are (you know this because you're reading this book). So make them...even if it means exploring the "P" word.

Your passion is what gets you going. It's what drives you—and your choices—every day. It's the force *behind* your choices—what you will do, who you will be, whom you will be *with*. Many of us don't think about our passions a lot. Some don't think about them at all...have never thought about them. Even when we're curious about our passions we often put off giving them some good, hard reflection time. Many of us have somehow learned along the way that passions are for later, that we can figure them out when we've gotten our work done, when our to-do list is complete. Even when we know what our passions are, we don't necessarily integrate them into our lives. They become something we play with on our rare off-hours, perhaps on a weekend.

Not the way to go...if you want bliss, anyway. Your passion is for you to live 24/7. In every piece of your life stew.

Every. Single. Piece of it.

My blissfuls do this, though they acknowledged it hasn't always been easy.

Many talked about needing to stay strong when living a passion-focused life, because so many people around them took great pleasure in chiming in with their opinions. These people would go on and on about how my blissfuls should be doing things a different way, pursuing different positions, raising their families differently, finding specific kinds of hobbies that would advance them in some way.

As my friends across the pond would say, that's just rubbish. In the end, *your* passion is about what gets *you* going. It will be different for others, and so their opinions are simply that—their opinions. They hold no more weight than your own. In fact, their weight comes in significantly lower.

As one of my blissfuls, an employee in her 40s, put it:

> *"The fatal flaw in life is when we try to be too many things or do too many things for too many people. Our first commitment must be to ourselves so that we are happy. That's how we can give to others. You need to know who you are and do it full out."*

Perhaps you already believe this. Perhaps your issue is actually figuring out just what your passion is. I've got you covered.

We're going to do it right now.

To figure out your passion, you need to take a step back from your day-to-day life. You need to remove yourself from *life's traffic*—the frenetic thoughts in your mind, the go-go-go pace of your schedule, the autopilot way you have of chugging through your day without taking a second to consider if anything happening in your day actually makes you *happy*.

When you remove yourself from life's traffic, you can take a step back and ask yourself this sometimes very difficult question: *Just what makes me happy? For real?*

Why can this question be so difficult to answer? Because

we've been brought up with so many ideas about what *should* make us happy that we forget to think for ourselves. Or because our minds are so filled with life's traffic all the time that it causes us to lose sight of what new blissful options might even exist. Sometimes it feels as if identifying passion is like picking a random idea out of thin air. You try to figure out your passion and your mind goes blank. So you just grasp at whatever you can think of…perhaps whatever you've been told to think of.

If this is you, and asking yourself this question is too difficult or doesn't achieve anything solid, you are not alone. The good news is that you can begin getting to it right now.

BLISS BUILDER EXERCISE
Your Blissful Passions

The *Bliss Builder* steps below will help you figure out your passions. You might find yourself circling around a few different ideas at first, but you'll bring them together in the end.

Some exercises will take some time, so allow for that. This may not all be done in one session, and that's perfectly okay. As with all other chapters in this section, the entire set of *Bliss Builder* exercises in this chapter may be done on your own or at *www.bogusbalance.com*.

Each step will come with a bit of instruction. Do your best with your answers. Have fun. Play. Dream. Discover.

Step 1: What does bliss mean to you?
This first exercise is as straightforward as it gets, yet it will most likely take you some time.

There have been many points along the way (and there are even more to come) when you have learned the definition of bliss from the mouths of my blissfuls. Now it's time to explore how you define it for yourself.

So do it now. Truly think about it and answer the following:

1. What does bliss mean to you? What does living a blissful life look like? What does it feel like? Describe it in the way that will most energize and motivate you.

Step 2: Reflect on your values.

This entire process is about going deep within you. It's about helping you narrow down what matters to you personally...the things you hold dear, the core priorities you stand for, the ones you want to guide your life.

The exercise below, inspired by Barbara Stanny's wonderful book *Overcoming Underearning,* includes a list of values to get you thinking about what is most important to you (the answer, by the way, is not "all of it").

Begin by circling the values that matter to you from the list below. The list may seem long, and some of the words will feel repetitive. That's because different words will resonate with different people based on their experiences. You may find yourself thinking of words that aren't included. Feel free to add them in.

Achievement	Community	Friendship	Patriotism
Discovery	Integrity	Honesty	Seeing the world
Family	Success	Adventure	Influence
Knowledge	Advocacy	Brotherhood	Peace
Impact	Honor	Independence	Being generous
God	Leisure	Health	Humility
Charity	Self-discipline	Joy	Life partner
Love	Truth	Simplicity	Making a difference
Justice	Relationships	Kindness	Physical activity
Individuality	Travel	Leadership	Intimacy
Spirituality	Retirement	Time alone	Comfort
Authenticity	Parenting	Self-esteem	Fun
Learning	Being free	Growth	Power
Humor	Security	Faith	Activism
Creativity	Creating change	Beauty	Using my talents
Happiness	Freedom	Leaving a legacy	Innovation
Service	Dignity	Strength	Relaxation

Now, of the words you circled, pick your top 10.

Your next step is to narrow them down to five. Force yourself to prioritize and rank them from most to least important.

Make hard choices. Use these values as the foundation to make decisions in your life about how you spend your precious time…and with whom. Put them where you can see them. These are the values you are passionate about. These are the values that will help you prioritize what you must integrate into your stew at all costs.

Step 3: Get those priorities down.

We've talked a lot about how you can't have *it all*, but that you must instead determine *your all*. Which means making hard choices.

Well, my friend, the time has come to make them.

It's time to determine what parts of your life will have a significant presence in your stew, what might make up a smaller piece, and what really doesn't fit in there at all. Right now, anyway.

For this exercise you will use the form below to create a list of your various life components.

You will see that the list already includes a number of components we've been discussing up to this point: "my work/career," "my life partner," "my friends" and "my family."

My life stew components:
My work/career
My life partner
My friends
My family

_____

_____

_____

_____

_____

_____

In order to get a full picture of your stew, you now need to complete the list with your other current life components. Do some brainstorming about the other activities and relationships taking up time in your life right now. What are your skills and hobbies? Do you follow a spiritual path or practice? Is there anything you're learning to do right now? What about fitness, sports or exercise routines? Are there any other self-care activities you engage in?

Narrow down your additional components to the ones that are most important or prevalent in your life and add them to the list. As an example, when I did this exercise I included the following items that mattered most in my life: meditation, traveling, workouts, writing, reading and learning about wine. Feel free to remove any of the life components listed for you if they are not relevant to you.

Now that you have a list of the various components of your life stew, your next step is to rank them from most to least important. Your ranking is based on the priority each item has in your life, on what matters most to you.

Do this now. I'll wait.

––––––––––––

Now review your list. Much like the values exercise, this list will force you to think about what truly matters to you. It is meant not just as an exercise, but to truly guide you when it comes to making choices about how you spend your life. It's critical to your bliss.

As Johann Wolfgang von Goethe put it:

"Things which matter most must never be at the mercy of things which matter least."

So focus on what matters most and let this exercise be your guide. For instance, if work comes in above everything else but you still want a family, then you need to find a life partner who can help make sure family needs are met, because you will simply not be able to handle both with the same amount of time and energy. Or you must recognize that now is not the time to start a family at all.

If you put one of your personal interests above everything else, then you need to find a way to fit that into your life so that you can engage in it frequently, perhaps even seeking a career that integrates it. Even then, you might need to cut something else out of your stew to give it the time and space it needs... since it makes you so blissful. Remember, bliss is about being discerning and choosy.

If something comes in low, around the 1-to-3 range, then you might want to consider whether this is a fit for your life right now at all. There are no obligations here and your time is precious. That being said, it might be an activity that happens infrequently or takes little time and is perfect for you. The most important thing is to be honest, and to be willing to let go of the things that really don't matter much to you. Perhaps it's time to let go of something that used to matter to you and that you hadn't realized was no longer a priority. Until now.

One final note. If you didn't list a lot of fun or self-care items, then you might consider whether there is an important element missing from your life. As we've discussed, the time you spend in activities that feed your body, energy and soul will not just make you more blissful. These things will also make you better at what you do the rest of the day...not to mention a whole lot more fun to be around.

Step 4: What's the deal with your past?

While finding your bliss is certainly not about living in the past, there's much to be learned from your past that can help you figure out where you're going next.

You have a gold mine of information that will tell you what's worked—and not worked—for you before. And now you get to use it all for this greatest good, for the creation of your bliss.

This step involves thinking about the events, projects and people that have pleased you, made you happy, perhaps even delighted you in the recent or far-off past. It also means reflecting back on the events, projects and people that did not. Remember to be honest, to refrain from judgment.

Answer the following questions and, for this exercise, take a good amount of time with each one. Really think about the answers. Pull out your old calendar, emails or other tools that will remind you what's been going on in your life.

You can also pull out the journal you've been working on since you started this book, knowing that some of the responses (especially the ones dealing with the most recent past) might overlap with it. No matter. In fact, it's good, because it's helping you pinpoint recurring themes in your life.

1. Reflect on the past week...everything that went on, from your work projects to your recreational time to your appointments to your travels to your meals with others.

    a. What was your favorite part?

    b. What did you dislike the most?

    c. What left you feeling the most energized and excited?

2. Reflect on your past three months.

    a. What were your top three moments?

    b. What three moments did you dislike the most?

    c. What left you feeling the most energized and excited?

3.   Reflect on your past three years.

    a. What were your top three moments?

    b. What three moments did you dislike the most?

    c. What left you feeling the most energized and excited?

4.   Reflect back on your lifetime.

    a. What were your top three moments?

    b. What three moments did you dislike the most?

    c. What left you feeling the most energized and excited?

5.   Now...

    a. What do your favorite moments have in common? What are the themes?

    b. Of these themes, which leave you the most energized and excited? What are you most interested in? What are you most passionate about?

6.   What professional careers relate to the themes and passion above? What hobbies or personal activities relate to them? (Note: This is a good place to brainstorm a bit. Explore online job guides or occupation searches. You can also search the internet using your themes as key words or phrases, or ask your blissful others to explore ideas around your specific themes.)

7.   What do your least favorite moments have in common? What are the themes?

Step 5: What's the deal with your present?

This is where your journal—the one we just talked about, and the one you've been working on since you began this book—comes into play.

The journal is your assessment of your current life. By now you should be very familiar with the questions, and have a good sense of what provides energy and happiness to your days. And what takes away from them.

Review your daily entries and take notice of patterns that have arisen over time.

1. What do your favorite moments have in common? What are the themes?

2. Which of these leave you the most energized and excited? What are you most interested in? What are you most passionate about?

3. What do your least favorite moments have in common? What are the themes?

4. Which moments bring up the most negative energy or emotion?

Keep the journal close as you'll need it in just a little bit, when you work on your specific plan. Also, feel free to continue to log if you still need to get a sense of your current state of bliss (or lack thereof). Your bliss is a work in progress, after all.

Step 6: Embrace envy.

Envy is *not* a deadly sin…not in my book, anyway. Envy is a terrific tool to help you realize what you might want in your life… especially when you're not sure how to figure it out.

This step involves thinking about those you admire (whether people you know personally or those you admire from afar)… and those you decidedly do *not* admire. It involves understanding why you envy certain people—the jobs and relationships and things they have in their lives that you might also want in yours.

A few words of caution regarding envy. Envy as we're using it here is not about resenting people for what they have, or wishing that they had less of it so that you might feel better about yourself. It's also not about comparing yourself to others and coming out feeling like you are less valuable than they are. You're not.

This is about triggering ideas you haven't thought of before. It's about gaining understanding about what you might integrate into your life to make it more blissful…not because someone else has it, but because you could have it as well. You just hadn't thought of it yet.

Answer the following questions, and take your time on these. You may have more than one answer for each, which is fine.

1. Who do you admire professionally? Why?

2. Who has the best job in the world? Why?

3. Who do you admire personally? Why? What does that person's life have that you envy?

4. Who is in a relationship that you envy? Why?

5. Who knows how to do something, displays a skill, engages in an activity, plays a sport, regularly visits someplace or has something else in his or her life that seems interesting or like great fun? What about it do you envy?

6.   In general, is there someone whose life always seems to fall into place easily? Who knows what he or she wants and can get it without tons of stress or pain?

7.   What characteristics does the person listed above display? How does he or she live?

8.   Of all that you envy in the lives of others, what leaves you feeling the most energized and excited? What are you most interested in? What are you most passionate about?

Step 7: Narrow down your passions.

Once you've completed the first six steps and feel ready, take a look back at what you've written. Also take a look at your responses to the reflective questions in the previous four chapters. Specifically note your responses about what leaves you the most energized, excited, interested and passionate.

Recognize the common themes that have come up, and with them in mind, carefully answer the questions below. And take your time.

1.   What are some of your favorite activities, experiences or relationships from your past that you would like to integrate into your life more regularly?

2.   Which of these energizes and excites you most? Why?

3.   What are some activities, experiences or relationships from the past that you absolutely don't want making their way back into your life?

4.   What about your current life do you like the best and therefore might integrate more fully or often?

5.   Which of these energizes and excites you most? Why?

6. What about your current life do you like the least, and therefore might need to change, decrease or eliminate?

7. What are some new skills, ideas, interests or ways of living that you would like to begin integrating into your life?

8. Which of these energizes and excites you most? Why?

9. What would you like to never do again...ever?

Now, as part of this step of narrowing down your passions, complete the following sentences:

I know that finding my bliss means identifying my passions. As of right now, my passions include continuing or beginning to pursue the following activities, experiences and/or relationships:

I also know that some things and people take my energy away from my passions, and so I plan to make changes so that the following activities, experiences and/or relationships occur less or not at all in my life:

Well done, you!

You just did a lot of work and are well on your way to reaching your bliss. You've identified some things that you are or may be passionate about, and some things that you definitely are not passionate about. Excellent!

We have one more step in this chapter, and it involves putting together a specific plan to reach your bliss.

When I asked my blissfuls what bliss looked like to them so that I could create the *Bliss Bits*, I received one response that summarized in two lines exactly what we're doing next. It came from a couple, both recently retired from high-level positions and married for 42 years:

"What works for us is to A) identify what is important to us, B) prioritize those important things, and C) keep our eye on the ball."

So now you know where we're headed.

Before we get started, I want you to know that this next section—much like the steps you completed—will take some time and energy. I say this because I not only want you to be excited about it, but I also want you to have the time and energy to do it right. If you used a lot of energy in the first part of this chapter and feel somewhat depleted, then I suggest you take a break and come back to this when you feel ready. Trust me, you'll want to give it your all.

Go ahead, take a break. I'll be here when you come back.

PART II: LIVING YOUR BLISS

Welcome back! Ready to roll with your final *Bliss Builder* exercise of the chapter? Here we go...

Now that you've begun narrowing down what energizes and excites you, now that you have identified what you value and what will drive your decisions, it's time to get concrete. It's time to create a plan to achieve all of your impending bliss.

Before we get to it, one more note. As much as you're putting together your plan for bliss at this moment, the blissful journey itself will take a bit of time. It's pretty clear that racing to a new, blissful place tomorrow, walking away from the life and the commitments that are currently part of your life's traffic, isn't the best strategy. This may come as a relief since creating change—no matter how positive—can be challenging in its own right (more on this in the next section).

The journey to bliss requires patient, intentional work. It involves mapping out your journey from point A (where you are at this very moment) to point B (bliss) in a way that feels right to you, fulfills your obligations and creates constant, intentional, positive forward movement.

I say this phrase again: *constant, intentional, positive forward movement...*

...starting now.

Yes, now. Even though the journey will take some time, it begins now. This isn't about figuring out your passion and putting it in a drawer somewhere until you've decided you've earned it...or decided you're ready. You already have and you already are.

The journey begins now. Changes need to begin happening now. Why? Because now is all you have. Because you know you want to be blissful as soon as possible.

This next *Bliss Builder* session will look a bit different from the others. It's less a series of questions and more about creating a blueprint, a blissful path, breaking things down more specifically and doing it from your own point of view. It's time to commit.

Keep your values, your priorities, your answers to the various questions and the passions you identified close as you make decisions in the following statements. Be as specific as possible with what you want, and think about what you feasibly can achieve and what you will need to sacrifice along the way.

Let's get going...

BLISS BUILDER EXERCISE
Your Blissful Blueprint

My Blissful Life

1. When I achieve it, my balanced, blissful life will look and feel like this (describe it fully, including how it will feel, what you will be involved in, the people around you, any given blissful day, etc.):

2. The makeup of my blissful stew, including any career, life partner, family and various specific personal components, will include the following:

3. The components in the list above will be ranked like this:

4. Each component will take up the following approximate percentage of my time overall:

My Blissful Career

1. When I achieve it, my blissful career will look like this:

2. When I achieve this, I will feel this way about it:

3. I commit to reaching bliss in the area of my career by making the following changes:

4. In order to achieve my blissful career path, I will need to make the following changes in the next six months:

5. Knowing this, I will make these changes by the following deadlines:

(Add as many lines as you need to make your blue-print meaningful to you.)

<u>Change</u>   <u>Date</u>

1.

2.

3.

6. The first step I will take, which I will do within the next 24 hours, is:

7. Knowing that bliss is about having my all and making choices, I also know I will have to sacrifice the following in order to achieve my professional bliss:

8. Though it may be hard, I will go about dealing with these sacrifices in the following ways:

My Blissful Life Partnership and Family

1. When I achieve it, my blissful family life (to include my primary partnership) will look like this:

2. When I achieve this, I will feel this way about it:

3. I commit to reaching bliss in the area of my family life by making the following changes:

4. In order to achieve my blissful family life, I will need to make the following changes in the next six months:

5. Knowing this, I will make these changes by the following deadlines:

(Add as many lines as you need to make your blueprint meaningful to you.)

Change _____ Date

1.

2.

3.

6. The first step I will take, which I will do within the next 24 hours, is:

7. Knowing that bliss is about having my all and making choices, I also know I will have to sacrifice the following in order to achieve my bliss:

8. Though it may be hard, I will go about dealing with these sacrifices in the following ways:

9. I will thoughtfully communicate these changes to my partner and family in this way:

My Blissful Self-Care, Interests, Hobbies and Friendships

1. There are many self-care ideas that will help me relax, recharge and/or re-center. I am excited to continue to integrate them into my life, and will do so in the following ways:

2. When I achieve this, I will feel this way about it:

3. In order to achieve this part of my bliss, I will need to make the following changes in the next six months:

4. Knowing this, I will make these changes by the following deadlines:

(Add as many lines as you need to make your blueprint meaningful to you.)

<u>Change</u>   <u>Date</u>

   1.

   2.

   3.

5. The first step I will take, which I will do within the next 24 hours, is:

6. Knowing that bliss is about having my all and making choices, I also know I will have to sacrifice the following in order to achieve this:

7. Though it may be hard, I will go about dealing with these sacrifices in the following ways:

My Blissful Others

1. As I make these changes and continue on my journey to bliss, I will need support from others. The kind of support I will need will be:

2. When I have this kind of support, I will feel this way about it:

3. The following individuals will be part of my support team:

4. I will talk to them about being my support within the next week, and when I do so I will tell them the following:

5. I also know that the greatest support I can get is from myself. When I begin to feel doubtful, scared or guilty, I will say and do the following things to keep me on my own blissful path:

And Wow...

1. This is exciting! I am energized about this journey because I know it will bring me bliss in the following ways:

2. And when this happens, I will feel this way, because this is what bliss means to me:

Congratulations!

Not only have you decided it's time to achieve your bliss, not only have you explored what that blissful life will look like, but you've also made specific plans and commitments to get there.

I hope you're feeling energized and excited, because this is energizing and exciting stuff.

If so, great. Feel it. Take a moment and breathe it in and out. Can you feel the bliss beginning already?

Now, all of this being said, you will most likely experience a few moments that aren't quite so energizing, a few moments of fear or sadness about what this journey will mean. It's all natural and perfectly normal. You just need to prepare for it, and plan on how you will keep a hold of that brain so that it stays your blissful ally and doesn't become your bogus foe.

But not to worry. We are tackling that next, so head on over to Section III when you're ready and we'll get started.

BLISS BIT

*"Bliss for me means knowing that I made real,
positive contributions to those around me."*

BATTLING THOSE SNEAKY BLISS-BUSTERS

SO YOU'VE WORKED your way through the first two sections, you've created a blissful blueprint for yourself, and here you stand, knocking on the door of Section III. Well, come in, come in…I'm glad to have you!

There are a few important things to know at this point. First of all, you *will* have more bliss in your life from now on. You must. You're in too deep now, and bliss is forthcoming.

Oh, and you'll begin to feel balanced, too. For real. No longer will you strive for the bogus definition of balance, the one that sets you up for ongoing frustration and stress. Instead you will make choices that lead you to take your day in stride, smiling because you will be involved in things that make you happy, things that feed you, things that are true to what you want. Most of the time.

Hopefully you've already begun to experience it all somewhat, and that you've got a sense of how happy it will make you.

Now, as you work through your journey, as you implement the choices you've made and begin to make changes, it's not going to go perfectly. Nothing does.

You might find yourself doubting your decisions. You might find yourself scared. You might find yourself wanting to quietly tiptoe from the uncertain future—as blissful as you know it will be—and right back toward an unblissful, bogusly balanced life.

It's natural to feel this way, of course, but those feelings don't have to have all the power. You can decide to keep right on moving forward on your journey. This section will help you do it. It will help you build a toolkit to tackle those bliss-busters, those doubts and fears, and get them behind you so that you can continue forward to bigger, better bliss.

We'll begin with Chapter 10, which offers specific ideas and tips on how to make true changes happen—and then stick with them. Chapter 11 will further explore those brains of ours, how they have an uncanny ability to keep us stuck, and how we can change the wiring so that our brains become more help than hindrance. We'll then tackle the money issues and fears we all face from time to time, followed by chapters that cover a wide variety of steps, tips and practical ideas to keep you on your journey.

It will all create your bag of blissful tricks, which you can tap into whenever you want. You might use it a whole lot in the beginning, and that's perfectly fine. In fact, it's great. Because that means you're sticking to your blissful path.

And in the end, that's the most important thing you can do.

CHAPTER 10

Embracing the Big C

"If something doesn't work, try something else. Very few changes in life are permanent. Even fewer are fatal."

—BLISSFUL WOMAN IN HER 20S

WE BEGIN THIS section with the chapter on the Big C.

Change.

I appreciate you for joining me here, as I know the very word can be pretty scary.

Understandable.

The fear around change is perfectly normal. So are the other negative emotions you might find you're feeling as you begin to put your blissful plan into action. Emotions like doubt, sadness and grief.

Though we often think otherwise, feeling negative emotions is not a bad thing. Negative emotions are natural and necessary, just like all of the more positive ones. They allow you to know what's been holding you back up to now, to understand what concerns you. And if you allow yourself to feel these emotions...if you don't block them, if you don't struggle, if you just let them pass through you...then you will get to the other side of them more quickly.

The most important thing is that you don't let those negative emotions talk you into taking a U-turn, to a life that was decidedly not blissful enough for you. It's all about working *through* the fears and doubts and coming out the other side, remembering that you're doing what you need to do to get yourself to bliss, so that you can serve yourself and others in living a happy, more connected life.

After all, you're doing what so many of my blissfuls said was the most important piece to the blissful puzzle.

You're being true to you.

And, truth be told, you really have no choice about your impending change. Not if you want to be blissful. Now that you've realized you want to be blissful *now,* now that you have a working plan to get there, and now that you can picture how things are about to get so much better, the only option is change.

The other option, the one where you stay where you are, which is probably a little or a lot stressed, a little or a lot overwhelmed, and a little or a lot unhappy…a little or a lot of the time…doesn't even make sense anymore.

But Deirdre, I can hear you saying, *I really* don't *have a choice right now. I can't make changes in my life. I've got kids. I've got responsibilities. I've got* [insert your reason here]. *I want bliss, yes, but I can't make it happen right now.*

We've talked about the stories we tell ourselves. And sure, you have certain commitments today. As we talked about in the last chapter, nobody expects you to leap carelessly off the non-bliss cliff and land easily on the blissful ground below. It doesn't work that way.

But be careful. Since change as a concept can be so scary, we tend to have an incredible mental capacity to fight it with the stories we tell ourselves. (See Chapter 3.)

Make no mistake. Bliss can begin today. It doesn't have

to come to its fullest manifestation by tomorrow, but you can begin with a first step. With two steps. You have no reason not to. You *do* have a choice, I promise. So think about it. And be honest with yourself.

Because really, why in the world would you *not* want to be more blissful...starting now? That's our end goal in this short life of ours, right?

So yes...change we must!

The first step is simply knowing—and embracing—that change will indeed be part of your journey, that some of it will be scary, that you'll make some mistakes along the way...and that you need to do it anyway. You cannot get to a new, more blissful place in life without changing some of the things in your current life.

Resisting this notion is tempting. Change is so scary because it is so unknown. So often we hang onto the things we know as if our lives depend on it, because even if they make us miserable, we can control them. We understand them. There is no risk that comes with the unexpected. And—let's face it—it's often easier. Some of us cling to things because we know it will take a lot of effort to snap ourselves out of that unblissful autopilot we've been used to, and we just don't want to deal with it. Yet deep down you know that you must deal with it. You know your life doesn't depend on the known, on the unhappy things to which you might be clinging. Deep down you know there are things you can change, some of them fairly quickly and fairly soon.

I promise that many of the things you're hanging onto now, the things you feel you can't possibly live without, perhaps the people you feel you can't possibly ease out of your life...I promise they're not *everything*. They're just known, so they are comfortable. Secure.

But when you're on the other side of this, when you're closer to bliss, you won't miss a whole a lot of them. Perhaps you won't miss any of them. In fact, you'll shake your head and smile at all of the work you put into holding onto things that, in the end, weren't nearly as important as you thought they were.

So now that you know you've got to push through the change on this path, just how can you do it? Here are some ideas to get you started...

THE BIG C, STEP 1: ENVISION YOUR BLISS.

When your blissful plan creates any level of anxiety in you, when you find yourself talking yourself out of this whole thing, when you want to put this book down and read some trashy novel instead so that you don't have to think about it...stop.

Breathe.

And create a picture in your mind of what your life will be like when you find bliss.

Picture it in full color.

Imagine how you will feel. Imagine the smile on your face as you enjoy every single component in your stew. Imagine how your newfound bliss will energize those around you.

Imagine waking up in the morning and feeling excited about the day ahead of you, a day that will be made up of things that make you feel good. Imagine that even the mundane or unpleasant tasks in your day are okay because you feel happy throughout the rest of it.

Imagine feeling balanced, truly balanced, because your stew is filled with only the components that matter to you, because you're being true to you. Because you're living *your all*.

Imagine not sighing with dread or anxiety when your alarm goes off in the morning.

Imagine getting to the end of the day exhausted but fulfilled from all of the meaningful things you did, the things that fed you. Use these images to drive you when you feel doubtful.

Go back to your description of bliss from Chapter 9 and add to it. Write it up in full Technicolor. Draw a picture, build a collage, collect images on Pinterest or create something else that will help you stay grounded to your bliss. Keep it very close. Use it to remind you why you're on your path.

If you can't envision your own bliss, then think of those you know who truly are happy, perhaps the people you envy, the ones you listed in Chapter 9. Picture the general expressions on their faces. Their general tones of voice. Their temperament. How content they are. How they thrive in their own skin. How often they smile.

This will be you.

THE BIG C, STEP 2: GRIEVE WHAT YOU NEED TO GRIEVE.

We've talked a lot about choice. We've discussed how finding *your all* means sacrificing or saying good-bye to some things or relationships that you've always had in your life. In some cases you might be leaving behind something that was *good* in your life in order to find something that's *great*. And that can be harder than anything.

Saying good-bye to the things (and, possibly, people) you are leaving behind in order to get to bliss is part of the process. But no matter how good or bad they felt to you, they still represent a loss in some way. Chances are you will miss some of them. You might need to mourn them, to say good-bye and let them go. Allow it to happen. Allow yourself to feel sad or scared or frustrated at what you're sacrificing.

It might hurt, but again, hurt is not a bad thing. It is a natural part of the process, something you will get through. Grieve what you are leaving behind, then *leave it behind*. Picture it moving away from you, and you from it. Journal about it if that works for you. Know that you will be more than okay. Know that you will be blissful.

Know that as part of this process, your clever mind might turn your grief into regret, might try to get you to return to something that was not blissful for you. When this happens, you need to remind yourself why you took this new path in the first place (and ask your blissful others to remind you as well). After all, you made these decisions for solid, thoughtful reasons that aligned with your values and priorities...so you just need to remember them.

My blissful retired executive in his 70s dealt with the grieving process when he chose to leave his job, which meant dealing with the loss of the status and position in the community that he'd had for so long. For him, experiencing the feelings and then moving on to more blissful parts of his stew got him through:

> *"The change was tough. I was well-known in my field and it was easy to get swept up in that. When you stop, that ends real quickly. I took it hard. I was hurt and defensive. It's a natural thing. It takes time and expanding into other things in life like travel, cars, education. I got a life coach and explored things like acting and boxing, until I found what I liked. And then everything got better."*

Transitions are tricky. People will come and go in your life. They might act differently. Other things in your life might unexpectedly change as a result. But, in the end, you'll be happier. That's why you've chosen your new path and the changes associated with it.

Trust me. You *will* get through your grief. And then you can look back and wonder why you allowed yourself to stay stuck for so very long.

THE BIG C, STEP 3: KEEP IT CONSTANT.

The thing to know is that your journey is a lifelong one, and your blissful path should always be *happening* in some way. Every day. You should always be working toward bliss, making the changes you need to make, measuring what's working and what's not, reflecting every once in a while about how you're feeling about things.

This is your job for now. You don't get good at things by thinking about them when it's convenient, or when you've got other things out of the way. And you certainly don't want to tell yourself some bogus story about what else you need to get done before you've earned your bliss. You've earned it. In fact, you're long past due.

You get good at things by thinking about them constantly, sharing them with those you trust, celebrating each change no matter how small. This is something you should feel proud of. Release any fears of being selfish. Release all guilt. Enlist your blissful others to help you with this. A blissful life is what you deserve just by being here on this earth for this short time. And a blissful *you* will benefit everyone around you.

So get good at getting to bliss.

THE BIG C, STEP 4: BE MINDFUL.

When the bliss begins to seep into your life, you might not even notice it at first.

Sometimes your new level of bliss will sneak up on you. One day you might just find yourself feeling lighter, waking up with a smile. One day something that always bothered you won't bother you anymore. One day you'll realize you're living a more blissful life…and feeling more blissful as a result. Yes, it works that simply.

Recognize your bliss before it slips away, before your thoughts return to life's traffic.

Pay attention to your emotions every day. Be mindful about what new things matter to you today—the things you do, the conversations you have, the experiences you value—when they might not have mattered before. Be mindful about the things that no longer matter today, when you couldn't possibly live without them before. Be mindful about how you're feeling, the stories you might be telling yourself, the inventive ways you might be letting your journey take a backseat to your old life stew.

Being mindful, noting your own successes, your moments of peace and joy, along the way, will help you remember why you're on this journey. It will create momentum to keep you going. When you notice you're veering off-course you can then gently veer yourself right back on it.

Make your mindfulness formal for a while. Continue your journaling from the beginning of the book to notice what's working for you, what's not, and how you're feeling about it all. Reread your plan from the last chapter and adjust if needed. Use the worksheet in the appendix at the end of the book (and at *www.bogusbalance.com*) to continue your journey. Check in on how you might be changing, about the progress you've made... even if it's incremental.

Bliss will begin the second you decide to make it a part of your life. Sometimes you just won't see it right away. But, if you pay attention, you might find yourself feeling lighter, smiling more and/or not taking things so seriously,

I give an example here of a change that at first went unnoticed. Until it didn't. It's not from a blissful, but from me. Here it is.

I used to be a terrible, terrible *driver.*

I was dramatically impatient. I was a honker, *one of those people who get some kind of weird pleasure out of laying on the horn when someone cuts in front of them, or when someone takes a second too long to hit the gas when the light turns green. Once I began working on my bliss, I thought I'd be able to change this behavior by using some new tools…tools that reminded me to breathe, to get perspective, to remember what's really important.*

Then, one day, someone cut me off and I laid on the horn just a little.

I was shocked…not because I'd honked my horn, but because I realized how long it had been since I'd done it last. It had been months! And I realized how I felt after honking. I felt…well…gross. I realized it was a sign of anxiety and angst inside of me.

I realized that honking the horn was no longer something I did regularly, that I was no longer a honker…*and that this little honking incident was rare. It was a sign that things were actually way off that morning, that I was feeling anxious about my day and had unconsciously reverted back to an old pattern.*

I realized in that moment that my journey to bliss didn't give me the tools I needed to find bliss in traffic. Instead, I didn't need *the tools at all. Being more blissful meant I just didn't get cranky in traffic the way I once did. It meant I was more at peace more of the time. I realized that, for the most part, driving as quickly as possible to every destination while getting others out of my way no longer mattered the way it once did.*

That, I realized, was blissful change sneaking up on me.

It was a relief. For me, and no doubt for anyone else who had to drive near me.

THE BIG C, STEP 5: USE YOUR BLISSFUL OTHERS...AND STEER CLEAR OF THE REST.

You know why your blissful others matter. That's why you've taken such great care in identifying who they will be.

Now use them. Get them to keep you honest. Remember what you asked them to do, the kind of support you requested from them, and then stay true to it.

Remove all embarrassment or guilt that you're taking too much of their time. You're not. This is too important, and chances are they are delighted to be a part of this critical circle for you.

Besides, you'll return the favor to them if they need it, right? Perhaps you'll even motivate them to begin their own journey.

At the same time, resist bringing others into the fold if you've identified them as individuals who might do a bit of damage on your journey. Don't sabotage yourself by discussing your journey or challenges with those who won't be able to give you the support you need.

CHECKING IN...

So how are you feeling about change? Doing okay? It's all good. Just breathe any negative emotions out. And know that your fear isn't just normal, but also a sign that you're really committed to change...which means you're really committed to your own bliss.

I knew you had it in you.

CHAPTER 11

Getting a Hold of that Brain of Yours

---

*"Even when I'm really struggling, I know I'll figure
something out. I really believe this. I know it to be true."*
—BLISSFUL WOMAN IN HER 60S

OH, THAT BRAIN of yours.

So you've decided you want to have bliss. You've decided you actually deserve it, and so you've planned for it. You've figured out just what you want and the things and people you want with you as part of this journey. You're feeling great about things, if not a little scared. You've got your strategy to tackle change all worked out.

You're ready to take this journey on…

…and then your brain steps in. And it has other plans.

The brain is a funny, unique thing. It's also incredibly powerful…which is why I've given it its very own chapter. It's related to change, but it also brings with it its own special challenges, creating barriers to your bliss in its own special way.

To be fair, the brain brings a lot of good things into our lives. It helps us wonder and analyze and solve various challenges. It is our constant companion, our closest advisor, providing a never-ending flow of thoughts and ideas and critiques with dizzying speed. It never stops, continually supplying its steady stream of chatter throughout the day and, often, at night.

And this is the problem. The brain *never stops*. It doesn't let up. It doesn't give us a chance to breathe, never mind determine if those critiques, questions and doubts it came up with are real.

And those critiques, questions and doubts? They're often aimed directly at us.

We discussed this somewhat back in the chapter about how we make things more bogus for ourselves. You may have noticed then that many, many of those sneaky techniques involve the brain.

We've grown to trust our brains as being virtuous and our thoughts as being fact. There is no other voice in our lives that is so constant, that is always there with us, providing commentary with a definitiveness and an assuredness that makes arguing with it pretty difficult.

We believe our brains look out for us, stimulate us, provide for us. And this is true in some ways.

But.

Our brains and their continual commentaries also provide a constant train of doubt, fears and ego-driven critique. We see others and we size them up. We analyze them as good or bad, and then compare ourselves with them to determine our own worth.

Self-preservation is the name of the game for our brains. They make it their business to keep us alive and continuing on our current path with as little risk as possible. Which usually means to go with what we know, even if it's decidedly unblissful. As we discussed in the last chapter, change is often accompanied by constant thinking and wondering and doubting and worrying. And as we work to deploy our strategies to tackle change, our brains have an incredible ability to fight back.

Our brains can convince us we are superheroes or that we'll never be good enough. Our brains can tell us we're the smartest, most beautiful person in the world (we're not) or the stupidest, ugliest individual that ever walked the planet (we're not).

Because our brain's job is self-preservation, it is aggressive in its efforts to keep things just the way they are. It works hard to preserve our egos, our known existence...which means it takes seriously its role to avoid risk, to continue on a path that may or may not be good for us, simply because it's known.

It does this self-preservation work very simply, by continuing to inject fears, doubts and guilt into every moment. It plays to our egos, tells us we need to be better than others to be worthwhile. It negotiates, talks us out of taking a blissful step until we've accomplished something decidedly not blissful. It takes the steam out of our blissful train. It tells us we cannot take a step until we know for sure it is the right one. It tells us we cannot fail, for failing at something would make us failures at life. So we don't take a step for fear everything will fall apart.

The brain is great at guilt. It knows just which buttons to push and which words to use to get us to feel bad about putting ourselves first, to make us think we're being irresponsible, selfish, lazy. The brain can get desperate at times, saying things to us that we would never say to anybody else in the world...not even our worst enemies.

We sit down to make our plan for bliss and our brains tell us we need to first get the cupcakes done for our daughter's rally tomorrow. We decide to book that amazing trip we've been planning, but our brains tell us we're being selfish. We decide to find a new job because we know the current one is not feeding us, and our brains tell us we're being irresponsible.

Our brains can mess with every day...every moment, if we let them. Even taking a breath and going for a walk in the middle of the workday can become a momentous, selfish and irresponsible act according to our brains.

And so, since the brain has all of this power, and the brain can use it to mess with our bliss, it is up to us to deal with it.

We must make our brains our partners in this journey. Which means we must reprogram the way our relationships with them work. We must rewire them.

It's easier said than done, for sure. After all, we've relied on our brains for quite some time. We've spent a lifetime with them. And, yes, our brains have come through for us in many ways. But they have also held us back.

Changing the wiring means starting with what we know deep down, and what we have no problem telling others when they need to hear it. We tell people they don't need to do anything special to earn bliss, that they've already earned it simply by being in this world. We tell people that they are worth taking steps to make their lives happier. We tell people that mistakes are perfectly fine. We tell people that sometimes risk brings great reward.

We know all of this when it comes to others, but not, for some reason, when it comes to ourselves. For some reason we've got very different rules of life than everyone else has.

Which is completely bogus. The same rules apply. And we need to believe it. It shouldn't take any kind of special negotiation with our brains to decide we want to be blissful and get going mightily on our journey to get there. We need to help our brains get on the same page.

Which means taking the steps below. They'll seem familiar to you based on the work you've done so far, but are specific in dealing with the brain, arming yourself with the verbal weapons to take your brain on when it will seemingly stop at nothing to knock you off of your blissful journey.

1. GET SQUARE WITH YOU.

Remember this one? Well, keep it right with you, at the fore-front of your mind at all times. It's critical to battling the fears and doubts, the arguments about why you shouldn't risk los-ing your title or your money...why you shouldn't risk trying something new for fear of failure. Instead, you will know that no matter what kind of money or title or accomplishments you have in your life, you are a worthwhile, valuable, lovely person. Get square with you and get your brain on the same page.

2. GET PERSPECTIVE.

This is another critical one that we've discussed, one that will make all the difference as you overcome your brain's negative thoughts. It's about your ability to recognize—and remember—what's truly important to you. It's about your need to identify priorities based on what really does matter to you and to those you've chosen to share this journey with. You need to remem-ber this, to step outside of yourself and gently remind yourself about your greatest passions, and you need to do it as you would communicate it to a dear friend.

You need to take the long view, to remember in the moment that something that is stressing you out doesn't mean every-thing. In fact, it might not mean *anything* a few days from now. So don't get caught up in it to the point that it drives your deci-sions and your life.

To this point, keeping perspective is also about recognizing that we tend to blow a whole lot out of proportion when we feel stressed. All of a sudden a project that's taking a bit more time will become the thing that gets us fired. Or the moment our children talk back to us becomes a new trend that says they're on drugs, or we're a lousy parent, or both. Thoughts do not equal facts. It's natural to exaggerate in our minds. Just know that's what you're doing when you do it.

And know the truth about so-called crises, which is that they almost always pass without anything too serious happening. Know that one week from now, chances are you'll have moved on to another so-called crisis and the thing you're dealing with now will be a faint memory.

As one blissful, an entrepreneur in her 60s, put it:

> *"There's a peace that comes when you understand that there will be good and bad days. Even when things seem at their worst, I know it will be better tomorrow. And I know that in one month I'll have forgotten all about it."*

3. PAY ATTENTION.

In order to battle our brains, we need to actually recognize when they're giving us those harmful thoughts, the ones designed to mess with our journey and hold us solidly in our current, unblissful situation. Relentlessly and constantly pay attention to your thoughts, especially in the beginning.

Recognize when your brain is telling you stories about why you don't deserve bliss—or at least why you don't deserve it *now*. Recognize its various sabotaging strategies.

Your brain is wired to tell you certain things. Again, it does this not because it's bad, but because it's looking out for you, like an overbearing parent that wants you to survive. For so long the brain has not been about living blissfully, but just *living*, as long as possible. And, to be fair, it's worked. For a long time. After all, you're still here. You're just not blissful.

Not yet, anyway.

4. CHANGE THE WORDS AND PICTURES.

Once you've recognized the constant stream of fears and doubts coming your way, the next step is to continually switch your thinking. You must remind yourself that you will be fine no matter what happens on your journey. You must remember that fear of change is about fear of something that *may* happen in the future, some terrible consequence that your incredibly potent imagination has concocted for you and made real. Something that most likely won't happen. And if it does, you'll deal with it with everything you've got. Because you can. And, no matter what, you are fine right now.

You must remember that you are capable of change, that you deserve bliss and that you will deal with whatever you need to deal with as part of your journey.

I do a lot of visualization work when I rewire, picturing myself physically swatting away the thoughts that continue to pop up—the ones that judge others or myself, the ones that criticize and compare. I give myself something else to think of at that moment...a blissful picture of something I'm excited about, an upcoming event I'm looking forward to, or something in my life that I'm grateful for at the moment.

Remember in the last chapter when we talked about visualizing how life will be when you get to bliss? Paint that picture in color in your mind and keep it close by for just such an occasion.

Carry a reminder with you—a piece of paper with a supportive message on it, a rock, or something else that works for you—and use it to remember to pay attention. Learn to cut your negative thoughts off at the pass as they're happening. Change your habit, from letting your brain go negative to getting it to go positive.

Another technique is to come up with a few mantras or affirmations—positive statements you will say in the moment, when you need to turn your attention away from your old thoughts and over to something new and positive. Simple thoughts like "I am excited about finding my bliss" or "I am worthy and loveable right now" or "I can't wait for XXX to be a part of my blissful life" can be wonderful weapons against those negative thoughts. Find one that works for you ASAP.

Another idea is to think differently about your day and the various parts of it. As one example, instead of thinking of each day as a bundle of stress to untangle, one of my blissfuls, an employee in her 20s, likes to think of it as a puzzle:

"I look at each day and think about all that I want to do and how I can fit it all in. I'm constantly moving things around to make the puzzle work for me. And when things get out of whack, I know I need to start making boundaries again so that I can regain balance."

(On a side note, this blissful has another interesting strategy for creating boundaries at the office: she and her partner share a car. This means she is forced to leave work on time since she has to either catch the bus or a ride home with him. When her workload increases she makes accommodations, but for the most part having one car ensures that she and her partner get the home-time they want. It's just one more example of a creative way of living life on your own terms, for your own bliss.)

Getting back to our main point, when you break your old patterns of thinking, when you refuse to let those fears and doubts run your life, when you align your thoughts with all of the bliss this will bring, then you change the wiring.

An associate of mine used to say that "things that wire together fire together." When you begin to associate bliss with positive thoughts, it's not long before new ideas and change are loaded with possibility instead of terror. It's not long before bliss stops being about guilt or negotiation, and instead becomes something you know you deserve. It becomes something you know will mean you're not just living, but living happily…which will make the lives of those around you happier, too.

A FEW WORDS ON
THE BRAIN AND A-TYPES

If you are a driven, intense individual…if you are all about the goal, about pushing yourself to achieve new things at every turn, about winning at all costs…if you find yourself regularly thinking or saying phrases like "just suck it up," "there's no excuse for failure," "I'll sleep tomorrow night" or "I can't stop now, I'm on a roll," chances are you've got some A-type in you.

Welcome to the club.

Being A-type is not a bad thing. You get things done. People look to you as a leader. You achieve what you set out to achieve more often and—of course—more quickly than others.

But all of this can come at a steep price. The price of your relationships. The price of your health. The price, certainly, of your bliss.

I'm writing to you, my A-type readers, because I know first-hand how intense your brains can be, and how they will stop at nothing to push you to do more, more, more. I myself was a super-driver, pushing my body and mind to go farther and farther without looking within myself, around myself or back at anybody I might be leaving behind.

And while I'm still a proud A-type, I've realized how to take my intensity and use it when I want to…while easing up when I need to.

Several of my blissfuls are A-types. And, like me, they had much pride in what they had achieved and continue to achieve in life.

166

But.

They said it wasn't until they recognized the damage their intensity was causing to them and their loved ones—and then did something about it—that they were truly happy.

Had they achieved things before? Yes. Were they admired? Yes. Were they blissful?

Absolutely not.

And when they made positive changes to their lives, when they focused on what truly mattered, did they still achieve things? Yes. Were they admired? Yes. Were they blissful? You bet!

The thing to know as A-types is that our brains are especially crafty in their efforts to keep us moving forward at any cost, despite whether or not whatever it is actually feeds us, is good for us or makes us happy.

As an A-type I love my brain for lots of reasons, but I am also aware of its drawbacks. So I know that I have to pay more attention…to those stories, negotiations and messages about needing to prove myself (*all the time*) that pop up at every turn. And when they do, I need to determine what's real and what's bogus. I need to recognize what truly makes me worthy, what truly makes me happy and what my body, my life and my loved ones really need at any given time.

Then—and this is the hardest part—I have to do it. And that's when all of the tools in my toolkit come into play.

Awareness for A-types is the first and most important step in dealing with our brains, because those brains are so amazingly adept at convincing us to just drive ahead—often blindly—toward some kind of future achievement (that, chances are, will never be good enough anyway).

Remember the guy I talked about in the Bogus Bottom chapter? The one with all of the surgeries? He said being an A-type, which he referred to as a "driver," was behind much of his physical and personal issues:

*"It's hard to balance when you're driven. I would say that
I was selfish and self-centered before because being driven
to success was so important to me. We can all rationalize
that we need to work so hard because we're providing for
our family, but that's not the case. The truth is that drivers get validated by meeting goals, so that's what we do.
For drivers, you almost need a crisis to slow you down
and get you to stop. The question is how big will the crisis
be, and how will you come out on the other side?"*

This A-type did indeed change. He did indeed rewire his brain.
But only once his body broke down. Once his survival depended
on easing up on his life.

To be clear, this blissful is still driven, but his drive isn't
about *win, win, win* at all costs. He is much more discerning
with his time, life and priorities...which is what makes him
blissful today.

It makes sense for all of us A-types to listen to his question.
To heed his warnings. To practice the lessons we've learned and
follow our path. To keep perspective. To get square with us. To
do everything we can to keep our crisis small, and to learn as
much as we can so that we can come out on the other side with
a true sense of balance—and a real path to bliss.

We will still achieve things. Lots of things. But the things
we achieve will be things that matter to us, things that drive us
toward bliss...not away from it.

BLISS BIT

"The best answer I can give to define bliss is the intention statement I have pinned on my bulletin board...My deepest intention is to be completely myself, self-aware and self-realized, living my life joyfully and to its fullest capacity."

CHAPTER 12

Tackling Your Money Issues

"Bliss is not worrying about every penny I spend."
—BLISSFUL WOMAN IN HER 50S

AHHH, MONEY. It's such a seemingly simple thing...after all, it's just a piece of paper, yes?

No. Absolutely not.

Money isn't just a piece of paper. It's a piece of paper that stands for something. That stands for many things, actually. And it can completely mess with our blissful journeys.

In my book *The Mission Myth* I talk about how money is both good and evil. On the one hand it lets us do the things we want to do, representing comfort and security. On the other hand, because it does these things, it leads to the often paralyzing fear that a lack of it will equal a lack of those things. Which freaks...us...out.

The other problem with money—as we've discussed—isn't what it may or may not bring us, but what it may or may not represent *about us*. It represents our value and worth. Which, for many of us, makes the absence of money not just an issue of fear, but an issue of shame as well.

Because of what it represents, money is often a big secret. We don't talk about it with each other. We're sensitive about how much we have versus how much others have, and we determine whether we are better or worse than they are based on those amounts. Money brings us shame. Money brings us pride. Money brings us anxiety.

Money drives our choices in an unhealthy way, for unhealthy reasons.

Which is why we need to deal with our issues around money. Now.

Our very first goal when figuring out the money part of our journey is to understand the truth behind it...what money really means to us.

We need to be clear why money is such a tricky issue, and how it can drive our decisions and choices—perhaps driving our choices *away* from the thing we really want to do—in order to avoid the fear and pain and shame that comes with not having enough of it. When we take a better-paying job that bores us or deprive ourselves of experiences that feed us strictly because of our own money issues, we need to realize in the moment that we have lost our blissful way. When we make choices strictly because of money it messes with our priorities, values and passions...leading to decisions that leave us feeling stuck, inauthentic and incomplete.

Yet many of us do it, and it makes perfect sense in the moment. One need only consider the pressures in today's society to make *more, more, more*...because *more, more, more* means more, more, more *power,* more, more, more *success,* more, more, more *things.* Society mistakenly believes that all of this will automatically lead to more, more, more *happiness.* And all of it takes more, more, more *money.*

Money came up again and again in many of my interviews and focus groups. For many of those not yet blissful, the perpetual fear associated with it was noted as a sometimes insurmountable challenge...something that caused them to stay stuck.

My blissfuls, as you might expect, had a different perspective. To be clear, they valued money. They appreciated that money gave them the freedom to do the things they wanted in life, take care of their families and contribute to their communities.

The difference for my blissfuls was that they'd learned to get to a place where money didn't rule their worlds...or their minds. As we've discussed, it didn't identify them as people. It didn't determine their value.

As with everything else, there are no easy fixes to our money madness. But some themes did come together from my blissfuls on how they've dealt with that sometimes paralyzing money pressure.

I present them to you below.

1. GET SQUARE WITH...

...you!

We've covered this, so no need to go into the concept all over again...except to say that you must know how awesome you are no matter what you make. Because you are.

Now, at this point I think we know each other well enough that I can share how powerfully my own money stuff came into play because of this issue.

Suffice it to say I used to hate tracking my business accounting. *Hate* it.

As I mentioned, when I first started my business I was not square with me. This meant that those rare times when I actually launched my accounting software to check in on my numbers were dangerous in the Maloney house. I recall a specific day when the anxiety was at a peak level. I sighed heavily, clicked on the accounting icon on my computer, turned to Hubbie and said, "I need to let you know that I'm about to look at my business account and I am going to be very sensitive. So please watch what you say to me and understand that I will need lots of validation when I'm done. Oh, and I might snap at you. Please don't take it personally."

Wow, Deirdre, you might be thinking, *what a pain in the butt you are.*

I can't say I disagree with you based on this particular example. But I can say that it represents the exact circumstances that cause so many of us to go astray on our blissful journey whenever money comes into the picture.

I was sensitive because I was about to see—in quantitative black and white—just how much I had (or hadn't) earned in my business...just how much I'd contributed (or hadn't) to *team Maloney*...just how much I'd been of value (or hadn't). And it rocked my world. When the numbers were higher, I was higher. When the numbers were lower, I was...well...not much fun to be around.

I let the numbers stand for more than they needed to. Until, eventually, I got square with me. I'm still working on this issue to this day, but at least now the reconciliation of my accounts isn't quite so paralyzingly scary. Nor is it quite so dangerous for Hubbie.

2. GET REAL...AND PLAN.

Once you get square with you, then you're ready to actually look at your financial picture in a more objective way. You'll understand what money does and does not represent.

To be clear, I'm not out to vilify the dollar here. It can lead to certain amounts of happiness—not in and of itself, but because of what it might allow you to have in your life or provide in the lives of others. You just need to get real about it so that you can understand the role it will play for you and how it will be used moving forward.

To do this you need to take a good, hard look at your financial picture.

This entails more than simply checking in on the number in your bank account and feeling better about yourself the higher that number lands.

Instead, it's about figuring out your blissful gap and creating a blissful budget. Here's my little formula to figure it out in its simplest form.

- First...know what you really need in this life.

- Then...know what you really want in this life, above and beyond what you need.

- Then...figure out what your needs and wants together will cost over the next year. Break it down by month.

- Then...calculate how much money you will have over the next year. Break it down by month.

- Then...make a plan to fill the blissful gap, should it be there.

A few thoughts on this formula, which is by no means an exhaustive examination of your financial situation, but is instead meant to get you started on identifying your blissful gap.

When it comes to identifying something you need, you might want to follow up with this question:

Do I *really* need this...*really*?

You might find yourself thinking you need a certain amount of square footage in your home or that you need to save for your child's tuition at the most expensive university (just in case)...but are these the true reality? Are there other options, other ways to take care of your needs that also allow for more blissful wants in your life?

There are no right or wrong answers in all of this. And there is certainly no judgment here. This is simply about you thinking through what makes you blissful, what makes you happy in the moment but might not be worth the cost, and what just isn't of value to you at all. You'll also want to recognize what expenses you might be enduring because others are doing something and/or tell you that you should be doing it (to this I say, get over it…your money is worth more than that).

We often forget to go through this thought process, especially once our expenses become a habitual part of our norm. We think our expenses are all fixed when, really, just a few of them truly are.

Now, when it comes to what you *want*, let yourself dream. Let yourself think big and blissful. Get out your blissful plan and visualize your bliss. Think about how you might add in some more blissful elements to your life. And again, watch those stories you tell yourself…those excuses you make…those negotiations about getting blissful *later*. You may not be able to have all of the things you want right away, but you can certainly take steps in their direction. Chances are there are plenty of things that can get your bliss going that don't cost a fortune.

Prioritize your needs and wants, then objectively look at your income and create your blissful budget accordingly. Give some thought as to how you can save or spend differently to bring in the things that truly bring you joy.

The only caveat regarding your list of expenses—especially your wants—is to make sure the items are about contributing to your blissful life, not acting as a happiness substitute or some kind of numbing balm for the fact that you're not happy and don't plan to be.

Throughout the process, be honest and reserve judgment on your own needs and wants. And don't allow others to judge you, either. It's not their business.

The exception to this, of course, is if you have a life partner with whom you share finances. In this case, involving him or her in the formula, the exercise above and your budget is a good idea. The hope is that you can both do this with emotional strength and mental objectivity. Money is a tricky thing when it comes to life partnerships...especially because partners tend to have different beliefs about money and different wants around how to spend it.

If you can do this process together, that's ideal. If you need to work on your communication or dynamics first, then go back to the chapter on the blissful partnership, engage in other resources around strengthening your partnership and do this as soon as you can together. In the meantime, work on your financial plan as best you can.

My little format above may be super-simple, but it's nowhere near super-easy. That's because it doesn't involve just numbers, but also involves feelings. It involves seeing in black and white where you want to be and how much farther you have to go. It involves staying emotionally strong and mentally objective throughout this process, and knowing that whatever those numbers are, they are *not* about you as a person.

As you do this, it's extremely important to be realistic at every step. And to watch the stories you tell yourself. At every step.

Remember that this is meant to be a healthy financial process, once that lifts you to a blissful place. So be blissful, and be realistic. Spend on the wants that will make you happy while also leaving money for the rent.

One more thought on this, and it's the most important part.

If you're in debt, get out of it.

Face it for real. Know it's not about your worth as a person. Know that lots of other people are going through it right now. Know it's temporary. Know you can handle it. And get out.

Easier said than done, of course. I know plenty of people who struggle with massive debt, and the shame and depression and fear that come with it can be terrible. I've seen what it can do to someone's sense of well-being.

I'm not going to pretend to be an expert on how to get out of debt, and will just say that my experiences with several people have illustrated that debt leads directly to a lack of bliss. There are plenty of people who know more than me about getting out of debt, who help others and who write books that help others. So find them, get out of your debt and get yourself to a more blissful place. You can do it.

3. TRACK, BABY, TRACK!

I've often said that I'm not a numbers person. And, really, I'm not. You might be the same.

But that doesn't give either of us an excuse to skip the tracking of our progress once we've made our plan and begun our journey. Neither does our fear about seeing just how much money we have, even if we're still trying to get out of that place where it defines us.

Tracking our dollars is just as important—and empowering to our choice-making—as every other part of the path. If you don't know how to track your money, then learn. There are great, user-friendly accounting systems and great, people-friendly accountants. Both of these resources can help you learn how to track your finances against your blissful budget.

The numbers aren't there to scare you, to make you feel ashamed or to get you to march right off your blissful path. The numbers are there to inform you, to empower you, to help you make blissful choices…the ones that will get you to bliss, always with positive, forward, intentional movement.

4. KNOW THAT MONEY IS LIKE WATER.

Money is ephemeral. It flows in and out of your life. You make it, you spend it. Sometimes you hoard it all because of your fear that you might one day be without it.

While saving money to meet your expected needs and plan for the proverbial "rainy day" makes sense, hoarding money and continually depriving yourself of blissful experiences is taking it too far.

Money in and of itself does not bring pleasure. There is no such thing as staring at your bank statement for hours on end and feeling as though you spent your day in a blissful, fruitful way. Money can bring pleasure because of the experiences it allows you to create in your life and in the lives of others. Which means it needs to be spent in order to do so.

In a way, it's like the way we work with food. We need to eat it and we need to burn it in order to live. The trick is finding that balance between the two so that we are fueled for a healthy life.

The problem is that we face that nagging fear: the one that says that if we spend it now, that'll be all there is…it won't come to us in the future.

And sometimes our reality reflects this in the short-term. There will be times when you have more money in your wallet and in your account. There will be times when you have less. Going on a big vacation or buying a new house will deplete your savings quite a bit. It can be scary, which is a completely logical emotion. But if you're thoughtfully bringing in money in a way that brings you bliss, in a way that serves your passions and priorities, it will come back. And if it doesn't return for a while, you can make a new plan. You can make different choices.

Money comes and goes in our lives. If you work for a business, you understand this. If you own a business, you know it intimately.

The point to all of this is that when you make your decisions on your blissful journey, when you have planned well so that you are not putting yourself in heavy debt or in an overly risky position, your choices around money need to align with your values and your priorities. Money can be a scary topic, serving as the perfect excuse to scare you right out of doing something that you know will be more blissful in the end. Don't let it. Plan well. Plan to make steps toward your bliss and know that you are worth it.

Remember the dangers around the word *earn*? Be especially careful about that word in this context. Yes, you may need to earn a salary. But you never need to earn the right to spend it by getting to a certain level at work or making sure every single whim of your child is provided for first. You've earned it already by being here and being you.

Plan well, earn your money and spend it in the best way that works for *your all*.

Your first few blissful steps—and the money associated with them—might be teeny. But at least you'll be making them. At least you'll know that you're worth it. And when you do it, you will feel different. You will feel lighter. You will feel happier. And you will know deep down that you are worthy of that happiness.

You are, you know. It's just that sometimes you forget it.

One of my blissfuls, an entrepreneur in his 50s, said his greatest challenge around money has always been his anxiety related to getting that next client. But he doesn't let that dictate his life stew choices. Here's what he does instead:

> *"I address this by reminding myself that I've been there before and got through it, and I will get through it again. I tell myself* it'll work out, just buckle down and do work, even if you don't want to right now, and things will come around. *And they do. Always."*

5. STAY IN THAT MOMENT.

Once you've planned, once you've realized what your priorities are and determined how you will get to bliss, then live the journey. Save carefully. Save as you planned. But spend as well. Spend as you planned. Just do them both with care.

Take action. Live in the moment. When those "what if" questions of paralyzing fear come into your head, get rid of them, push them away like we talked about in the previous chapter.

Remind yourself that you are worth your bliss, that you have planned, that you will adjust your path as you need to, and then live. Those pesky, paralyzing fears are incredibly persistent. You've listened to them for a long time, and they will not go quietly just because you've decided that bliss is now something you want and deserve. So you must combat them directly.

Remember, fears are all about things you are afraid will happen in the future. Right now you are fine. In fact, you're better than fine. You're on the path to bliss. You're in a good moment now, and when that future comes…the one you've planned for, you'll handle those moments just as beautifully.

In the end, do what my blissfuls do. Keep perspective. Remember that the small stuff will come and go—and so will the money. In the end, it's our bigger, blissful choices on the path that matter. It's how we choose to spend our time and our energy and whom we choose to do it with that matter. No matter what the numbers in the account might say on a given day… if in the long run we decide we want bliss, if we consistently and authentically pursue it, if we prioritize and plan and live, then in the end we'll know that we've experienced the journey that we deserve. And we will have brought amazingly blissful energy to those around us who get to share in it.

In the end, that's what true wealth is all about.

BLISS BIT

"My bliss is being able to go out with friends, family or my wife and not have the conversation drift constantly to my work or my stress about the things I have or don't have. It's about being able to be present with them and not focused on the project I'm working on, the meeting I need to schedule, or the report I haven't yet written. There's something about being able to shut off, knowing full well that you'll pick up right where you left off the next day."

CHAPTER 13

Live. Test. Repeat.

"You only go around this world once.
Make sure you go all the way around."

—BLISSFUL MAN IN HIS 60S

THERE ARE JUST a few more points to cover as we get ready to move past our theme of sneaky little bliss-breakers. These points are all designed to keep you firmly on your blissful journey track.

Because that's what you're going to do, yes? Of course, there will be moments when you stray, when you doubt. Perhaps a week will go by during which you haven't made any progress— or have even chosen not to think about the changes coming on your way to bliss.

But.

You will return to your path. You will. You must. You've already decided that balance—*real* balance—is what you want. You've decided that you want to be happy, peaceful, joyful, content. You don't want to stress out every moment of every day, trying to balance society's unattainable ideal of *it all*.

You've already decided that bliss is your future—a lovely, happy, light part of your future. The one you've already earned just by being who you are right now, this very moment. So that part's over. Now you're marching forward.

Below is a three-step process to keep you marching strong. When you get scared, when you feel bogged down...look at your plan, remember your values and remind yourself of these three steps.

Three simple steps. You'll be doing one or more of them at any given time, always toward and into bliss.

These three steps are your path. So follow them.

1. LIVE.

As you make changes, even the small ones you begin to make right away, live your newfound bliss with everything you've got. And enjoy it.

What does it mean to live your bliss? A quick review:

- If you've decided your job is a high priority, then make sure you love it! Settle for nothing less than something you enjoy, that fulfills and feeds you. Settle for no other boss than one who respects you and values your priorities...or, if you're an entrepreneur, be your own boss but be as fair to yourself as you would be to others you manage. Remember, drive and ambition aren't bad things. Not at all. Just make sure that the job itself feeds you, and that you're not striving for money, a title or a position alone...that your job is not simply there to stroke your ego or because you (or others) think you should be in it. Know what level of structure you need—whether it's flexibility of time and creativity or something more regulated—and look for it. Seek out what you want until you get it. And don't feel guilty. Your bliss will be your reward, and you'll be better at everything you do. You won't be sorry. And neither will those around you.

• If you've decided your partner and/or family is your priority, then make sure you make time for them, and love that time! Settle for no other partner than one who can support your needs, or at least stay out of your way while you get them fulfilled elsewhere (if that is what you decide is right for you). Seek out what you want until you get it. And don't feel guilty. Your bliss will be your reward and you'll be better at everything you do. You won't be sorry. And neither will those around you.

• If you've decided your work and your partner/family are both high priorities, love it all! Just remember that you can't have it all in the traditional sense we've all heard about, the one that puts all kind of pressure on us to do everything perfectly all of the time. Discover *your all*. Decide ahead of time on the right mix of professional/personal components for you, and find jobs and loved ones with which that will work. And don't forget to add other learning or fun adventure opportunities for yourself if that's what you want. Know that to have both professional and personal lives that are valuable to you will mean making sacrifices all around at some time or another. Know that they will overlap in your stew, and so pick components that will work well together. Be careful and thoughtful when choosing your jobs, partners and life mix. Don't set expectations you can't achieve. You cannot be perfect at everything. Seek out everything you want in *your all* until you get it. And don't feel guilty. Your bliss will be your reward, and you'll be better at everything you do. You won't be sorry and neither will those around you.

The most important thing you can do as you live your life is to be honest with yourself about—as one blissful put it—"what makes you tick." This is about what will make you happy, not about what you or others think you should be doing.

Make your choices based on your own blissful priorities. Otherwise the choices you make will not be the ones that give you true balance, true contentment in life. They won't make you blissful. And then what will be the point?

2. TEST.

You've done your best in putting together your blissful plan, but as you live it you'll find that you'll need to adjust. Getting to bliss will not be a perfectly sequenced journey. It will be messy, but in a good way. Because it means you get to play a bit. Messiness, with all of its triumphs and mistakes, is part of the ride. And no matter what, every decision you make, every step you take on your path, will help you grow. Every step will give you information as to what will and will *not* work for you, providing a wisdom-building, expansive, invaluable part of your journey.

The important thing is to know up front that it's not possible to make every change perfectly the first time around. And that's okay.

As you consider or take on new opportunities, you can always look at the first period of time as a test. We like to get in a big rush to figure it all out immediately and find some stability. We want to make the changes and settle in for a long, long time. Resist this temptation. As one of my blissfuls, an entrepreneur in her 50s, said:

"Don't be in such a hurry. Take your time. Sometimes you need to experiment to find the right thing."

When you make a choice and a change that doesn't work out as you'd hoped, know that it's part of the process. Don't convince yourself that you're now stuck in a new unblissful situation forever, nor use it as an excuse to go back to living your old bogus life.

Hear this. You're not stuck. If you want to make a change, if you want to find a new job or get involved in a new relationship or join a new group or try a new hobby, then by all means do it...and know that very few things are permanent. You can and should adjust as you go. Testing is about learning what is right and wrong for you, so that you can adjust toward your greatest bliss possible.

Testing can happen all of the time. Before you take on a new field, you can volunteer for an organization that focuses on it. Before you join an expensive golf club, you can try out several lessons with a few friends. Before deciding to start a novel, you can attend a conference or a writing group to feel it out...or just write a chapter or two. You have time, and it's important to make sure your choices of job, projects and people are the right ones for you. So test, and adjust. And be blissful all along the way.

One of my blissfuls, a business owner in her 60s, said she believes that people make permanent-seeming decisions far too soon in life. She believes that those living in their 20s should be all about testing, to see what they like and what feels right, to determine what makes them comfortable in their own skin and what makes them thrive, so that they truly get to know themselves before making bigger life decisions.

Many of us are past our 20s, of course, but no matter. Life is still about change. So test. *Get to know yourself.* Even those big, committal decisions can go through a testing phase. Want to get married to someone who seems like the perfect mate? Get to know the person well beforehand. Want a baby? Perhaps volunteer at a daycare or take care of your friends' children for several days. These are just a couple of ideas. In the end, your tests and how you go about them will be up to you. And while testing won't always be perfect in telling you exactly what you need to know, it's a great way to start.

In the end, most of life is a test anyway. We take a job hoping it will work out, but it's a test that sometimes shows us this job isn't right for us. We get married hoping it will work out, but it's a test that sometimes shows us this person isn't right for us. We join an association, take on a hobby or begin a project hoping it will work out, but it's a test that sometimes shows us the group or venture isn't right for us.

Notice I didn't use the word *fail* in any of these scenarios. These tests aren't the pass/fail kind. They are the kind that help us hone in on what really matters, what makes us comfortable, what makes us happy in our own skin. Tests are a way of getting to know ourselves. We're not always going to get it right the first time around. And we don't have to.

3. REPEAT.

Another critical step in keeping your bliss over the long term is to regularly reflect on the journey itself, and whether or not it still works for you the way you've laid it out. This means that every so often it will be worth it for you to reevaluate your priorities and your life stew.

One of my blissfuls, a now-retired employee in her 60s, talked about her need to continually reevaluate her priorities throughout her life:

"I had to keep double-checking what was important to me as a wife, a mother and a career person. There are a lot of people who will encourage or discourage you from your path, and so I had to take the time to think about where I was headed next and what I wanted to do. For example, at one point I focused on being a stay-at-home mom, and then at another point I knew it was time to move forward in my career."

Like this blissful, you will want to check yourself, to ask yourself tough questions. What is driving you today that is different from yesterday? How might that impact the choices you make about your job, about how you function within your family? What has worked and where have you gotten stuck? What can you do next to move forward toward your bliss?

I remind you here that I have included an appendix at the end of this book (and at *www.bogusbalance.com*) that lays out a list of questions to this effect and in a more formal way. Use it on an ongoing basis as an official check-in. Add other questions that will help you determine not just what steps you're taking toward bliss, but what new changes you're now committing to. I recommend completing this document three to four weeks after you complete the book, then again every few months in your first year. You'll want to continue using it at regular periods of time to check in. (And as I said earlier, I also recommend doing what I do, which is to conduct a total blissful checkup by completing all of Section II at least once each year.)

Remember, bliss is life's journey, not a specific destination that you'll reach and then check off the list. You will always be evolving. You must. It is part of a blissful life to continue to learn and experience and discover. As you evolve, so will what you want in life. It doesn't mean the changes you made before were wrong. It just means your bliss will be found in different ways now.

It might be that you're like the blissful above, that your kids are now grown and you'd like to focus on your career more than in the past. Great. It might be that you didn't think you gave that much credence to a management position, but now you've found that supervising people is extremely fulfilling, so you want to pursue a move within your company. Great. It might be that you've found that singing at karaoke is so much fun that you want to take professional voice lessons. Great.

The important thing to recognize and embrace is that life is ever-changing, and so are you and your wants. New opportunities will present themselves and new lessons will be learned. It's all okay. It's all part of the blissful journey. Nothing is constant. One of my blissfuls, an employee in her 50s, put it this way:

> *"It's important to take the long view. Your life is not going to balance every day. Work and personal stuff will need to take precedence at different times. It won't be consistent. If you really look at chapters in life there are times you need to pay attention to one over the other. And that's fine."*

So update your journey. Make a new turn on the map. Continue to play and seek out what makes you tick without guilt. Continue to adjust. Bliss is something not just for the *you* of today, but for the *you* of the future. It's for every single day of your life. The fact that it will change and evolve is part of the fun. So make sure every part of this lifetime is blissful.

And enjoy the ride.

BLISS BIT

"I experience bliss all the time...like when I am home on a Friday night, knowing that I don't have to go anywhere the next day. I have my favorite people with me, my husband and my son and our two dogs. Laughing, playing, not thinking about anything stressful and knowing that there is no place I would rather be at that moment."

CHAPTER 14

A Few More Blissful Tips

"Every consequence comes from a choice that I have made."
—BLISSFUL WOMAN IN HER 40S

BONUS TIME!

This chapter covers a few more bonus tips—an even 10, to be exact—on the art of getting and staying blissful. Some may sound a bit familiar, but they were critical enough to my blissfuls that they deserved some extra time.

Let us begin.

BONUS TIP 1:
COMBINE WORK AND PERSONAL LIVES.

Some of my blissfuls tackled the division of the components in their life stew by not dividing them at all. In fact, they intentionally combined them.

Here are a few examples from my blissfuls:

- An entrepreneur who created a co-working space for women included as part of her business the opportunity for her members to get together for social events through-out the day, as well as on evenings and weekends. She sees it as a win-win: she gets to run her company while also feeding her social needs by connecting with women she respects and enjoys.

- A man in his 20s who enjoys and values his position in local government also volunteers for and sits on the board of several community organizations. By doing this he meets other people with similar priorities and passions in life, develops new contacts and skills, and also gets to use his own experience to advance the issues that matter to him.

- A man and his wife, both blissfuls, both own their companies. They also both have their own, separate offices at their home. This allows them to do their work while also spending break time together and getting support from each other throughout the day.

Now, while I believe creating components of your stew that comprise both your professional and personal interests makes a lot of sense, I will also add a caveat.

Be careful when you mix your work and personal lives. Do it intentionally and with necessary boundaries. Combining your life into a stew does not mean you go out and get drunk with your direct reports at work. It does not mean you have a personal love affair with your boss. And you might want to think twice before starting a business with your spouse. It has to be right for you and your bliss…and shouldn't compromise your efforts or lead to bigger problems.

BONUS TIP 2: BUILD UP THAT GUT.

One interview question I asked my blissfuls was how they go about making tough choices...how they decide between a work and personal component when the two conflict, when both require their attention at the same time. I wanted to learn just how they know the right decision when a work opportunity conflicts with a family obligation. I wanted to know their process, if they weighed things out a certain way.

I expected a wide spectrum of responses, including answers involving cost/benefit analyses, perhaps a quick cerebral scan. But I didn't get any of that from my blissfuls. Instead, every single one said that when it came to making a decision, to making a choice between opportunities...heck, to just knowing that a choice they were making was right in the first place...*they just knew.*

As one of my blissfuls, an employee in his 40s, put it:

> *"I know instantly and at a gut level what the priority should be. If there's a thought process there, it's instantaneous."*

This response represented a sentiment I heard over and over again from my blissfuls. Each of them just seemed to know in their gut the right move to make at any given time...the move that would bring them toward bliss.

It was admittedly a bit frustrating for me, as a person who loves to offer concrete steps to success. Building your gut, after all, does not contain a quantitative formula. But, alas, this is what they said.

They said they didn't have to think long and hard when they made their choices—specifically when a work and personal component collided—because it came down to just *knowing* the best decision at the time.

Yes, they had their baselines. They knew their blissful stew, what a given day or week should generally entail as far as how they spent their days and evenings, as far as what amount of time they wanted to give to different life components. They also had their own priorities, so some of their choices would skew toward work commitments first and others would skew toward personal commitments first.

The point is this. When a conflict arose in their plan, when different parts of their stews were at odds, they just *knew* what should take priority at that time. And so they went with that choice, often without a moment of doubt.

My blissfuls had strong guts that did more than help them make choices during all of life's traffic. Their guts also meant that they *just knew* when it came to finding the right position, the right circle of friends, the right partner...and when the time came to make a change on their journey.

How nice for them, yes?

All of this leads to the blissful tip that we need to learn to tune in to our intuition, to build up our gut. As much as our head loves to weigh things out and chew on problems and challenge every decision we make, we need to let the head go at a certain point. We need to learn how to not just know, but *feel* within ourselves when a situation is right or wrong for us. Sometimes this feeling is extremely faint. Sometimes it rings loudly. Sometimes we know it's there but choose not to follow it because we really hate whatever it is that it's trying to tell us.

My dad got this. When I chewed on a problem and asked his advice, his answer was often in the form of a question:

"What does your gut tell you?"

I wasn't quite sure of the answer in the beginning, so I began to tune in...to listen to my gut and at least hear what it had to say when I made decisions. And when I went against it I usually regretted it.

Begin tuning in to your gut. If you're unsure of what to do, just wait quietly for a sensation from within you. It's there. Begin with something easy, something that requires a choice but isn't emotionally loaded for you, like which movie at the theater will be best for your mood and energy or what your body is truly craving for breakfast. Ask yourself on an intuitive level what would be best, then *listen*. Tune in to it. Tune inside yourself. It might be a quiet little voice at first. It might not tell you what you want to hear. But the more you listen, trust and act accordingly, the more your decisions will reflect who you really are and, therefore, what you really want in this life. Which is bliss.

Your gut knows you best. It won't steer you wrong, because it has every incentive not to. After all, it's a part of you. And it's not like the brain, which is about self-preservation. Your gut is about living a truly balanced, honestly blissful life. So when you listen to it and make choices as a result, you are being authentic.

Chances are building your gut will take some training, the way you might train a muscle to lift a weight. That's okay. Begin working on it, testing it out. You don't need to do it perfectly. In fact, you can't. So go easy.

You won't be sorry.

The blissfuls aren't.

BONUS TIP 3:
GET PERSPECTIVE...BEFORE YOUR CRISIS.

We've already touched on this a bit, but it bears repeating here because it came up so often, and was so important to my blissfuls.

One of my blissfuls, an employee in her 50s, told her story about learning lessons and getting perspective this way:

> *"One of my greatest challenges actually happened recently, when my mother became very ill and was dying more than 1,000 miles away. While I could work*

remotely, my ability to focus on my work during this time was very hard. The way I coped was to work when I could, which sometimes meant between midnight and 3 a.m., or while she napped. I attempted not to lower my standards but allowed myself to have some things be delayed, move deadlines. I also sought help from people. What I really learned is that it's important to help each other out. So much that we struggle with isn't life-and-death. Postponing a deadline at work might not make a difference, but putting off the things you need in your personal life could. I also learned to be more thoughtful about how I spend my time and create boundaries. Now I say yes when I mean yes, and no when I mean no. I always thought I was good at that, but having hit the wall, I now evaluate my availability and the costs of doing something a bit differently."

This blissful learned so many important lessons by getting perspective through her pain. The hard thing is to learn those lessons and get that perspective *before* the pain. Before you have any regret.

As I write this, I am hyperaware that this is another thing that is *so* much easier said than done. I wish I had a magic mantra or even some kind of pill to give you (and me) to help us remember to find and keep the long view. To help us realize each and every day that life is short, that we need to focus on what matters to us, to embrace it with everything we have. We need to remember that things will happen—bosses won't understand us and customers will irritate us and family members will disappoint us. But, in the end, a whole lot—almost all of it—doesn't really matter. And we need to focus on what does. Life is short and life is now and life is for the living. This means that *not* focusing on the big things—finding a job you love and living with a partner you love and creating a life stew you love—is a big, silly waste of your limited time.

We all know it. There are motivational posters to this effect everywhere. Yet each day we get caught up in life's traffic. It's natural.

It goes back to the idea of the bogus bottom. For some reason we think we understand the need to keep perspective, but it really doesn't happen until a crisis forces it on us. Only then do we remember that life is indeed short, that we are fallible, that we can indeed get hurt and fail, that indeed we are imperfect. And, most importantly, we remember that if we just stick to what we value and love most in life, in the end we'll be okay.

Do your best to take your values—the ones you identified in Chapter 9—seriously. Do your best to pursue your bliss and your dreams *before* you hit a bogus bottom. Create reminders of what you love and why you love it and why, more than anything else, these things are worth your time. Get it on paper. Carry it around. Think about what matters first thing and last thing in your day.

Know that nobody—and no life—is perfect, and that if you let too much time go by not being true to you, damage can and will be done. It's just a question of when and how bad it will be.

I say this not to depress you, but to help you get your perspective now...and hold it tight.

Yes, no matter how closely you stick to your blissful plan, bogus moments will happen. Bogus *bottoms* may even happen. But the more you keep perspective, the more you safeguard yourself, the more you give yourself the greatest chance at bliss for the greatest amount of time.

Just how important to my blissfuls was this notion of keeping perspective? So important that they brought it up continually, repeating it over and over. I include just a few of their specific quotes on the topic here:

- An entrepreneur in his 50s:

  "Don't sweat the small stuff. There are so many frustrations that happen in your work world that impact your mood and personal world, and it's a matter of keeping perspective. Don't let cranky people and little things affect you. So many things don't matter."

- A media professional in her 30s:

  "Don't let a life-changing event like having a baby or finding out your dad is sick make you think about what's really important in your life. You should just do it now. You should do it on a daily basis. If you don't, if you just get into your daily grind and you're unhappy, you'll find yourself stuck there."

- A marketing professional in her 50s:

  "Take the long view. It's not going to work perfectly every day...just know it will all balance out in the end."

- A business owner in his 60s:

  "Remember that life is finite and before we know it, families are grown and gone. Careers are important but could end tomorrow and you'll wonder if you spent your time on the right things. Work has benefit because it's tactile, you can see progress and you'll get accolades. It's easy to lose sight. Try not to."

BONUS TIP 4:
GRATITUDE, GRATITUDE, GRATITUDE.

We talked about this in the chapter about the blissful life partnership, but I wanted to be sure to bring it up here as a general rule for everyone every day.

It's a rule my blissfuls live by. They discussed it repeatedly, this need to be grateful about the people and things that made their lives so happy.

Granted, it's easy to be grateful for those who make your life blissful when your life *is* blissful. But even as you're getting there, even when things get messy with your choices…heck, even right now, there are things in your life that *do* work. There are people and things and opportunities around you that are positive, and they're only going to multiply now that you're on this journey.

While my blissfuls always looked at their lives through a lens of gratitude, they especially did so when things *didn't* seem to go their way. When negative emotions came up, many intentionally switched them to ones of gratitude…gratitude that they had support during their challenges, that they were breathing air, that they were surrounded by nature. They chose what mattered to them most in life and hung on to it tightly when they needed it most.

As rough as life can get—and I know it can get rough—there's still plenty to be grateful for. Sometimes you just need to sit down and force yourself to think of what those things are, especially if you are so stuck in the muck of life's traffic that you've forgotten.

That's what my blissfuls did—and do.

This is not about living a motivational poster. This is about what really works to create a blissful life for yourself. This is about a choice: the choice of gratitude.

I end this tip with two blissful quotes.

The first comes from a blissful, now in her 40s, who had been a stay-at-home mom. She talked about the difficulties she faced back when she was a new mother:

> *"...what made me happy at that time was knowing that there could be so much more stress in my life, and there wasn't. I didn't have to balance a paying job with being a parent. I didn't have a husband who worked 10-to-12-hour days or traveled a lot...and he was hands-on when he got home. I knew I was lucky."*

The next one comes from a corporate business owner in her 50s, who has often found herself struggling with a fear of failure:

> *"I can get so critical of myself, and it really gets in the way of my own happiness. One way I deal with it in the moment is to know I'm blessed. I have a fabulous husband, great kids, and a wonderful set of family and friends. I have a brain that lets me do my work. I am so grateful, and I try to keep that perspective."*

BONUS TIP 5:
KNOW THAT SELF-IMPROVEMENT IS NOT A DIRTY CONCEPT.

The good thing about this journey and its tricky challenges is that we've all faced them at one time or another. *All of us.*

What this means is that lots of people have figured out how to overcome their challenges effectively. Some of them have written about it, have produced videos about it, conduct workshops on it. And they are all available to you.

If this last paragraph caused some major eye-rolling on your part, just hear me out.

First, I understand your hesitation. There are plenty of well-deserved clichés about self-help gurus standing on a stage and trying to motivate you to find your passion while serving their own egos and wallets. Got it.

But.

There are lots of well-intentioned people who have been through their own pain and learned their own tough lessons and very much want to help.

You might be thinking that *of course* I would say this, since I'm writing this book. But that's not why I can state this so definitively. The reason I can state this so definitively is because I myself have been helped tremendously by some of these people—men and women alike whose stories I can relate to, whose styles of support and sharing work for me.

Many are speakers and authors I don't even know, but it doesn't matter. They are people who are authentic most of the time, who keep their egos in check most of the time. Their wisdom and lessons have been invaluable to me and continue to help me regularly. Even those resources that offer just one nugget of support or a new idea that resonates with me are worth my time and energy.

Self-help tools cover a wide variety of topics, using many different styles, formats and tones. When done right, they will help you feel validated and motivated. They might also ask you to take a somewhat painful look inside and find specific techniques to help you evolve. But that's how you'll grow, yes?

Let yourself consider self-improvement resources. Take some time to explore what topics, speakers and writers might work for you. Look at conferences or groups formed in your own community. Don't go into them blindly. There are plenty of reviews to read and people to ask to get a sense of the experience that awaits you, so consult them. Make sure this will help, not harm, your process.

You may also decide you want to find individual help on your journey through a coach who will support you through your various twists and turns. Great. Just make sure it's the right coach for you. I had a coach for quite some time and it was a terrific partnership. Before our partnership was solidified I interviewed several people, got lots of recommendations and made my choice carefully. Like everything else, being intentional about my choice and knowing what would work for me proved to be the most important thing.

BONUS TIP 6: REMEMBER TO...

...always be true to you.

Do not forget this one.

My blissfuls all believed this tip wholeheartedly. They believed it was the key to real balance, to true bliss.

One of them, an employee in her 40s, said it this way:

> *"Go after what you want with purpose and energy. Ask yourself what you believe you're supposed to be doing in this life. Knowing what this is and going after it makes it so much easier to make choices, to say 'no' when something doesn't fit. It also helps others to know what you stand for, and when they shouldn't even bother asking you to do something that goes against it."*

I can't overstate how often my blissfuls stressed the importance of being true to you...of knowing what you want, going after it authentically and living it with everything you've got to get to bliss. It is, they said, what will make you happy.

A few wise words from another blissful in her 60s:

"Follow your heart and your passion. Don't do anything for money...do it because you love it. And always honor the things in your life that you most love and value. I weigh everything against that which I love most in my life. I've always known what they are. In my case, it's my loved ones. If I fell over dead tomorrow the companies would go on and I'd be replaced. It's my family and friends that matter. I try to remember that always."

BONUS TIP 7:
THE COURAGE BEHIND BOUNDARIES.

Here's the other thing that happens when you're true to you... and square with you.

You realize that you don't need to do it all perfectly every time. In fact, you realize that you need to just show up to the things that matter to you and do your best in the moment. You realize you are not irreplaceable or indispensable, and you are fine with this. You have an abundance mentality, wanting to share your ideas and opportunities with others because you believe this will lead to your greatest successes and happiness. You do not fear the success of others because you know it in no way reflects on what you can and cannot do. And so you applaud them. You help them. And they do the same for you.

When you feel this way about your life and yourself, you know that you are worthy, that you don't need to do everything for everybody every step of the way. You are able to delegate without feeling vulnerable in any way.

You are able to set boundaries. You know it when the time has come to say no to something that is above and beyond what you've agreed to, something that won't fit in with your current workload, or something that will distract you from your other commitments in life.

As one of my blissfuls put it, you have the *courage to say no* when something isn't the right fit for you.

I love this notion that saying no is actually a sign of courage. So often we feel that setting a boundary or saying no will illustrate weakness. My blissfuls clearly feel differently. Yes, they know that setting boundaries is challenging. They know it can be scary, because it might disappoint someone or cause that person to think we don't care. It could hurt a relationship with someone if that person doesn't understand why we are setting the boundary in the first place.

It is because of these potential consequences (which often don't happen, by the way) that saying no is so courageous. We don't know how others will take our boundary-setting, yet we know we must do it anyway. Because we must stick to what will work for us, what we've committed to already and what we have prioritized in our blissful stews.

A blissful working mom in her 30s found this courage after she had her first child:

"Saying no to things used to scare me. I felt like it could jeopardize my job, like I wouldn't be valued as an employee. Now my perspective has changed. I still want to do a good job, but I also know that I just can't say yes every time my work beckons. So I don't."

BONUS TIP 8: FLIP IT AROUND.

We've spent a lot of time talking about the changes in your life that will lead you to bliss, about how you can plunge ahead on the change trail despite the uncertainty that awaits you.

While this is critically important, there will also be times when you need to stay in a certain unblissful, frustrating, annoying or otherwise negative circumstance before that change can happen...or for even longer because the negative thing is small compared to the benefit you get out of the overall situation.

When this happens, my blissfuls say it's important to flip things around...to take the negative thing and change something about it—or your mindset about it—and make it better in some way. Nobody is stuck, but you might just feel that way if a negative aspect of your life looms into the future for a while. So it's up to you to figure out a solution.

Here's a great example from one of my blissfuls. A high-level executive in the academic world, she found herself on a long and frustrating commute every morning and evening. She hated it, but she knew it wasn't going to change because she loved both her job and her home so much. So she decided to flip the situation around:

> *"Because of technology and my Bluetooth, I've turned this situation into something that works for me. I call people. I try to call one of our 150 employees and say something nice. I also call my extended family members who live far away. Because I'm stuck in the car I actually talk to them now more than I used to. It's actually made me closer to my aunts. I had to turn something negative, something that drove me crazy, into something positive."*

When something negative will be a part of your life for a while, flip it around somehow. Get creative. There may be ways to take a work schedule you hate and speak with your boss about changing it. There may be ways to pay someone to do your tedious paperwork if you sacrifice the cost of one spa treatment each month. There might be a regular spreadsheet you hate to review that you can now think of as some kind of brain-teasing puzzle.

You're not as stuck as you think you are, so brainstorm solutions and get your blissful others to help you.

BONUS TIP 9: BEWARE OF FOMO.

While the acronym FOMO (Fear Of Missing Out) may be somewhat new, the concept certainly isn't. Many, many of us find ourselves committing to events, staying late at work, or obsessing about being with our kids every second because we have a fear that if we step away, we might miss something.

Sometimes FOMO has to do with the fear of missing out on something fun. Sometimes it has to do with the fear of missing out on an opportunity…the chance to connect more with the boss, the chance to finish a project perfectly instead of delegating it to others, the chance to meet that special someone by showing up at every singles event every single night.

Two of my blissfuls, both A-type, driven male employees, gave me the same exact line as they told me why, in the past, they tended to work longer hours than they needed to:

> *"There was a part of me that just needed to be part of the action."*

I get it. I love action, too.

The problem is there will *always* be action—or the potential for action—going on somewhere. There's always the chance that the big call from your potential client will come in while you're at a family dinner. There's always the chance that something super fun will happen at your brother's holiday party, even though you've committed to be on the other side of town with your in-laws. You simply can't be there for it all…all of the time.

Sure, FOMO may get you to a new opportunity. But it can

also lead you to make decisions that aren't true to your blissful journey, decisions that might just drive you away from the happiness goals you've set.

Note that the first word of this acronym is *fear*...and fear, as we've discussed, is about something that *might* happen in the future. In this case it's about something that might happen that you aren't a part of. That needs to be okay. You simply cannot be a part of everything. It's not possible. There are too many things happening in life all at the same time.

Remember what my blissfuls said about living in the moment. Be happy with where you are and experience it fully. Sure, things will happen when you're not around. Yes, you will miss out on things at some point. But, if you follow your gut and your blissful journey, it won't matter. Because what you decide to do instead will be worth it, too.

BONUS TIP 10: GIVE BACK.

It's really quite simple. My blissfuls get blissful when they bring bliss to others.

This came up over and over and over again. My blissfuls talked about finding satisfaction, meaning and true happiness while giving of themselves in some way.

While my blissfuls certainly contributed money to some causes, this particular point was not about the dollar. It was about the giving of their time, their expertise and their compassion for their fellow human beings. It made them feel useful. It made them feel purposeful. It gave them perspective. It gave them gratitude. It took their focus off of their own life traffic and set it squarely on someone else for a while. Many identified giving back to their community as one of the biggest and more important pieces of their life stews.

One blissful told me that he is the man he is because of his community involvement. Another said that getting up in the morning and feeling like she has meaning, that she's improving the lives of other people, leaves her feeling blessed every day. Still another said:

"I feel good when I've done some good."

I wrap up this point with one last quote on the matter, this one from a blissful entrepreneur in his 60s:

"When you watch those that have been helped, when you see the smile on their faces, then life is blissful. Because for the moment, the feelings that overcome your entire body, mind and senses are fantastic...warms the cockles of my heart just thinking of it."

You've got to love this guy, yes?

BLISS BIT

"Bliss is having a job that provides me challenges in an environment where I am allowed to thrive, combined with a loving family I can come home to at night, and a close group of friends that share my passion for life. It feels like I'm always busy—but not to the point of exhaustion or burnout."

CHAPTER 15

The Science of Bliss

"There's a need to create habits and rituals."

—BLISSFUL WOMAN IN HER 60S

UP TO THIS point we've focused on a whole lot of art—the vision, the strategy, the priorities, the tips to reaching bliss and staying there.

In order to fill your toolbox with as many tools as possible for this journey, we need to incorporate not just art, but also science. As one of my blissfuls said, sometimes getting focused and dealing with stress isn't about some broad, mind-changing technique. Sometimes it's about a simple, practical change you can make to your day, to your schedule.

Sometimes these more science-y, practical changes can be just what you need to take that next step on your journey.

My non-blissfuls actually discussed the pragmatic side of this journey a lot, hoping to find the right tools and ideas to help them get to bliss. My blissfuls, of course, had already figured out some practical ways to assist them along the way. Below are some of their ideas...

1. GET A SYSTEM THAT WORKS FOR YOU.

Your system is your machine. It's the way you organize your life, the tools you use to juggle your life stew. It's the way you make sure you are getting things done—accomplishing what you want, when you want to, in a way that keeps your stress levels low, your energy high and your life balanced for real.

Chances are that the central piece to your organizational system of life is your calendar or planner. Or perhaps it's the to-do list or the smattering of sticky notes. Or the online program that rings a bell every time there's a deadline looming, or the notebook that holds a running list of projects, phone numbers, dates to remember, favorite quotes, shopping lists...et cetera.

There are countless options to organize your life. Here's just one example. It's my own system, which focuses on an Excel spreadsheet and a paper planner. The planner lays out my monthly calendar, providing a wide-angle-lens view of my life, one where I jot down my various appointments and meetings. The Excel spreadsheet is my to-do list, which includes an overall list of business projects and personal items broken down by category (speaking, consulting projects, business operations, my blog, my book, etc.), where I fill in my upcoming tasks and deadlines related to each. This spreadsheet also includes a daily to-do section. At the end of each week, I take all of my projects and tasks for the next week and assign them to specific days. At the end of each day I look to the next one and schedule my tasks and meetings into specific timeslots, taking the opportunity to think through my energy and assigning everything in a way that will best set me up for success. When the end of the day comes, I take what I didn't finish and move it forward to another day.

Again, this is just an example, and the most important point is that this is what works best for *me*. The trick is figuring out what works for *you*, figuring out what will not just help you achieve the things you want and need to do, both big and small, but do so in a way that will work for your personality, that will *aid* you in your journey and not stand as one more pressure-filled roadblock that makes you all tense. This journey is about feeling accomplished and excited, as well as being comfortable on a regular basis. Remember, we are at our best when we are thriving in our own skin.

A system can make or break that thriving as much as anything else.

Are you a list person, or does just the idea make you break out in hives? Does writing things down make your list feel more doable, or does your smartphone app create a better sense of control and peace of mind? Does the ringing bell signaling an impending deadline work for you or against you?

These things may seem small, but they're not. It reminds me of a terrific quote from Muhammad Ali:

> *"It isn't the mountains ahead to climb that wear you out; it's the pebble in your shoe."*

The wrong system can be the pebble in your shoe. You could have the best job possible for you at the moment and still find yourself struggling, stressed out and distracted because your organizational tools are all wrong for what you need.

Be honest about who you are and what you need to succeed while comfortably thriving in your skin. Think through what's worked best for you in the past, and beware of well-meaning people who tell you that their system is the *best one ever*, that you can't *not* succeed if you integrate it, too. They mean it when they say it, but it's not true.

The truth is, it's the best system for *them*. *They* can't not succeed. You're a whole different person, on a different path, with a different way of being in the world. And you need to set yourself up for your greatest success.

One more thing on your system. Beware of any mindset revolving around the magic solution—the one that will get you organized once and for all. Like health and happiness and... well, everything else, there are no magic solutions. Here's a quick tale to illustrate my point.

I once attended a seminar about organizing your life. I was seated with my boss at the time, a lovely, creative, somewhat chaotic guy who was constantly missing deadlines. Right before lunch, the seminar turned into a hard-core sales pitch, focusing on the company's book-like planning system to organize your life, complete with a series of cassette tapes to tell you how to use it. (Yes, cassette tapes. It was a long time ago.)

The second we took a break, my boss joined dozens of other people at the product table to purchase the very fancy system for about $400. The next day he proudly showed me his planner, all laid out the evening before with perfectly typed labels for the different categories of his life. He used it for about a week; then it became too big and bulky to carry around. He didn't update it and began to feel overwhelmed by it. He continued to miss deadlines regularly—and felt worse than ever.

Of course, there wasn't anything wrong with him. There was just something wrong with the system he chose for himself, because it wasn't the right fit for him. Instead of helping him it became one more shaming, stressful pebble in his shoe.

2. MAKE YOUR TECH WORK FOR YOU.

Whatever your best style and system, chances are technology will be a part of it in some way. You might not even have a choice—it could be a part of your work office culture, which might require that everyone use the same email and calendar system. Or it might require you to use a special company cell phone that doubles as a computer, GPS and accounting system.

This could make organizing your life a bit tricky, since you'll have both work-required technology and the organizing system you've designated for yourself in your life. When this happens, you need to integrate them together as best you can. For example, if your office requires you to keep all appointments updated in one digital office calendar but you work best using paper, take the extra step to do both if that helps you stay on top of your blissful game. The thing you need to do is to thoughtfully integrate your tech and your multiple systems in a way that will set you up for success...not more stress.

The other way to make your tech work for you, not against you, is to find some discipline around it. Remember what we talked about earlier regarding email and social media. Deep down, as much as we bemoan the way technology has inundated and overrun our lives, we love it. We love how it connects us and distracts us. We are compelled to check for messages or other signs that we are liked, important and part of a group.

Because of this integral passion, technology holds an immense amount of power over us. It can be hard to find the discipline to keep it from getting out of hand, to keep it from ruining our focus...on the projects we are working on, the people we are talking to or our own, blissful *us* time.

Discipline doesn't come from gritted teeth alone. Part of your designed system, therefore, needs to include the measures you will take to have and enforce discipline around technology. Simply telling yourself that you won't respond to emails while giving your kid a bath or sitting at a red light might not—probably won't—be enough. Switching your phone from a ringer to a vibration to keep from distracting yourself in a meeting might not—probably won't—do it either. Instead, you might need to turn off the *new mail* alert, shut it down, or leave the phone somewhere else altogether.

Let the people around you know about the boundaries you've set for yourself. Ask them to help you find success by calling you on it when you yourself begin to weaken.

You may just need some help keeping yourself honest on this one.

3. GET THE RIGHT PEOPLE WORKING FOR YOU.

One of the things my blissfuls emphasized was the prime importance of getting the right people working for you.

This is different from what we've discussed in previous chapters regarding your support system...your blissful others. This is literally about getting the right people to work for you.

Whether in a traditional office setting or, in the case of entrepreneurs, managing staff and contractors, hiring the right people is critical to not just achieving your goals, but doing it happily. If you have an administrative assistant who forgets to tell you about a meeting with an important client, you will not be as successful, you will feel frustrated and you will wind up spending all kinds of time keeping an eye out for what that person might be missing next. If you have an accountant who is constantly failing to get you the reports you need on time, you will not be as successful, you will feel frustrated and you will wind up spending all kinds of time keeping an eye out for what that person might be missing next. If you have a daycare provider who forgets to give your child medicine at an appointed hour...well, you'll just freak out and worry all the time.

We are nice people and so we like to give others a chance. And that's fair. We are also busy, tired, stressed and hate conflict. So we often let people work for us—poorly—for far too long. We let people with terrible skills or, just as damaging, terrible attitudes stay on when all they do is make things harder. We make a lot of excuses to ourselves and so we carry on, doing both our job and the job of the other person. And we feel resentful to boot.

Don't. The people you hire to help you in any part of your life need to be the right people, with the right personality and style, that you need to be successful.

It begins when you hire them, and with how you do it. Don't make hires blindly. Carefully interview every person you hire for any reason. Don't just hire somebody because it's a politically correct move. Get referrals and look people up.

Remember the point about testing. When you find a good candidate, share your excitement about recruiting the person, but also consider letting him or her know that you see the first month or so as a test so that you both can decide if you are happy with the partnership. Plan a date to check in and have a conversation as to whether or not the partnership is working.

Yes, the partnership. Everyone you pay to do anything you need is indeed a partner, one who can often make or break your bliss. So treat each person accordingly. Treat those who help you on your blissful journey with a lot of appreciation. Reward them. And when it's become clear that a person isn't the right partner, that the person has become a pebble in your shoe, end the partnership as quickly and fairly as you can. No excuses.

4. FIND YOUR STRESS SOLUTIONS.

As hard as you work on your bliss—the big art stuff and the smaller science stuff—the inescapable fact is that stress will happen. It's natural. It's part of being on this journey, where, despite your best efforts, the unexpected can sometimes seem more frequent than the expected. And it can stress you out.

Dealing with stress is another area where small things can make a big difference. Of course, it's all about finding practical solutions that work for you—that will lessen your stress, lighten your load, loosen your shoulders back down from your ears and, perhaps, even lead to a smile or a laugh about what it was that was stressing you out in the first place.

The first thing is to pinpoint what it is that tends to stress you out. We all have different triggers, and nipping the stress in the proverbial bud before it happens can be helpful.

Pay attention to when you feel stressed—to what incidents, what people, what times of day, what days of the week are part of the pattern. Notice what the real triggers are. They might be different than you think. For example, you might think your husband failing to pick up the mail on his way in the door is what's stressing you out...but it could be the real culprit is that you've been cooped up in your home office for hours, feeling isolated and alone.

Once you know the triggers, plan to address them. Make changes that prevent the triggers, be mindful of how you're feeling when the triggers are happening, and know ahead of time how you will deal with them when they do.

As part of my bliss-search, I conducted two focus groups with female entrepreneurs in all stages of their lives, their business and their journey to bliss. Though I'd left the questions open-ended without a chosen subject for discussion, the topic of stress took center stage for both groups.

In each group we brainstormed specific ideas to deal with stress, and they work for either gender.

I share them with you now to get you to think creatively about what might work for you...to think of new ideas that will make you feel more peaceful in those stressful moments, ideas that don't involve turning on trashy reality TV (though, to be fair, it does work in some cases. I know this firsthand).

This list is not exhaustive. There are plenty more ideas to deal with stress and some might work for you. But this is a good way to get started. (You will want to brainstorm your own ideas as well, and may find that the self-care activities you came up with in the last section can also be used for this purpose.)

So, in no particular order, here they are:

- Take a walk...Getting outside and spending just a few minutes getting the blood pumping can work the stress out, or at least lessen it.

- Read...For those who felt stress at night and experienced trouble sleeping, this one worked well. One woman said she always kept a novel on her nightstand. It was a treat for her because she spent her days reading books about business and history, and fiction felt like more fun.

- Get a hobby...In this stew of life, getting outside of the stress and tedium that often accompanies the workday can be addressed by finding a hobby that takes you out of your head, allows you to be creative without an end goal and introduces you to new people and energy.

- Volunteer...The benefits are much like those above, but with the added plus of helping you feel pretty good about your altruistic self. Volunteering also helps develop skills and make connections, combining various life stew elements as described in the previous chapter.

- Get a pet...Focusing on others who will love you unconditionally is pretty special, provided it doesn't lead to more stress. Just make sure you think this through and know it's the right solution for you. (I once owned the cutest puppy on the planet...for six days. I won't go into the trauma here, but know it was a pretty bogus week.)

- Imagine...This is similar to the method we discussed in the chapter about dealing with change. Let yourself dream. What will you feel like when you've gotten through the thing that's stressing you? What will you feel like when that big project or hard conversation is behind you? What will you feel like when you are truly balanced and blissful? What will the world look like? What will your breathing be like? How big will your smile be? Fully imagining that lovely place that awaits you can be quite the motivation to get there as soon as possible.

- Journal...Purging your emotions on the page for nobody to see can be extremely cleansing. Let yourself express what you're feeling with absolutely no judgment. Don't try to create beautiful writing at the same time. That will ruin your process for this purpose.

- Meditate...Giving yourself permission to not think at all sometimes feels like a luxury.

- Exercise...Sweating, getting the blood pumping, meeting new people, feeling good about yourself...there's a lot of good stuff here. Just pick a kind of exercise that you like. The last thing you want is to have this be another dreadful task to tick off your list, then feel miserable about yourself because you didn't get it done... because you dreaded it.

- Do nothing...and enjoy every minute of it.

When you look back at the list above, it becomes clear that many of the strategies suggested involve ways to deal with those racing thoughts that are constantly buzzing through our very busy minds…the ones that remind us how many things we have to do, the ones that warn us how many things might go wrong, the ones that tell us that we are not good enough, the ones that are based on fear and paralyze us.

In reality, many of the suggestions above are more about distracting ourselves away from these thoughts, more about changing the mental channel, than about dealing with them head-on. But, to be real, sometimes that's just what we need.

Now, a funny thing seems to happen when we find a stress solution that works for us. It somehow becomes too good, seems too indulgent, makes us feel like we're being irresponsible when we do it, so we avoid it until we feel we've earned it.

Earn. There's that manipulative word again. Several of the women in the focus groups brought this up…this silly negotiation game we play with ourselves. We will allow ourselves to do the things above, but *only after* we've gotten this or that done.

Sure, setting up a reward after doing a task well can be very effective. But remember to be careful about how often you use the words *earn, deserve* and *reward*.

Please hear me when I say that *you do not need to earn any kind of self-care or peace that you want to create in your life.* You have earned it already, just by being here on this planet. Life isn't about keeping your eye on the prize so you can get things done. Life *is* the prize. And it's short.

So live it…and beware. If you're one of the many people with long to-do lists, you'll find that the bar where you feel you deserve a break to take care of yourself will get higher and higher until it's unreachable. Sooner or later you'll find you're not taking that walk or reading that novel or going to the gym at all. Which only leads to more stress…and less bliss.

A few more quick points on dealing with stress…

Once you figure out what triggers the stress and what works

best in dissipating it, create habits and rituals for yourself to make sure you don't have to come up with a fresh new strategy every time. Set up breaks at the right time for you each day. Shop for the right breakfast to create the energy you need. Decorate the right space in a way that motivates and soothes you. While finding new solutions to stress can be fun, sometimes making new decisions or picking from lots of options will only add to your stress…so eliminate that possibility by preparing for those stressful moments before they come.

Which leads to my final point here…planning. Once you know your triggers and your solutions, don't leave things to chance. Be honest with yourself, and have your toolkit of options and phrases and people at the ready when the stress happens. Don't wait for the stress breakout to try to figure it out. If you do, chances are those shoulders will stay tensed up for a whole lot longer.

5. GET OUT OF HERE…LITERALLY.

One of the best ways to find true bliss in your current space is to get the heck out of it.

Just about every one of my blissfuls talked about the importance of traveling. Whether heading to another city, state or country, getting out of your space has the beautiful effect of getting you out of your own world, the world you've built safely around you, as well as getting you out of your own head. It actually seems to open things up in there, to create perspective on not just what's going on for you in your part of the world, but for others in their parts of it. It can be a very powerful (albeit humbling) experience to recognize that everything you've got going on is by no means everything that *is* going on.

The world is a big place, though the communities we build for ourselves can get very small. When we surround ourselves with the same networks and people and tasks and routines, it all begins to take on a level of grandeur and importance that isn't real.

To be clear, yes, your life is important and grand. But it is not everything. And when you step away, you not only realize that your life is just one way of doing things…you also recognize that there are ways of being and eating and interacting and speaking that you never even thought about. Because you haven't been exposed to them before.

My last point stated that routines and habits are a nice way of dissipating stress, which is true when it comes to your day-to-day. But there are times when shaking it up and exposing yourself to new things can be extremely refreshing. It can get those creative juices flowing around new ideas and opportunities. It can also give you appreciation for all of the amazing things you've got going on in your own hometown.

Take some time to not just take the day off, but to get *away*. The whole idea of using your precious two weeks off to get the house-painting done or spend afternoons at your favorite park are fine, but they won't give you that precious, mind-expanding, breath-refreshing perspectives that have made such a difference in the lives of my blissfuls.

The way you choose to travel will be up to you and your interests and your budget. As with everything else we've discussed, the important thing is to make sure that whatever you choose is what will serve and feed you…something you will truly enjoy. If your friends are backpacking through the Andes and tell you that you *must* join them—but you really like/need your hot showers and rest—then don't do it. If your kids want to go to Disney World but you know that other destinations will enthrall both them *and* you, then consider those options as well…or plan to take a day or two out of the week to do something that will leave you just as energized as they are.

Some of my blissfuls chose to save up their vacations and take them for extended periods. Some chose to do them for a week or so at a time. Some went on guided tours. Some went on solitary explorations. There are thousands of options out there. Begin exploring how you will explore—and don't stop until you find an option that makes you tingle and smile just at the thought of it.

I will end with one more brilliant point made by one of my blissfuls, who said she heard this piece of advice from someone she happened to know, someone who was blissful as well. This person believed that people shouldn't wait to travel—shouldn't wait to begin exploring the world—until the latter part of their lives. Thanks to this whole idea of earning our rewards and waiting until the bliss of retirement, many of us think this is the right way to go. Yet I think we all know there's a whole lot to learn right now. There's a whole lot to explore right now. And our mind could use a bit of refreshing right now.

So don't wait.

Go.

Now.

6. AND WHEN YOU GET BACK...

...have a sanctuary to return to.

One of my blissfuls said this was the single most important tip she could offer when it comes to living a blissful life. Knowing that stress is a part of life for everyone, she said that having a physical place to go to, one where you feel comfortable and safe and relaxed, can mean everything. It is where you refresh yourself, reenergize yourself and rediscover the bliss that may have disappeared for a while.

Here's more from her:

"I'm so blessed that my home is my sanctuary. It's quiet and nature is there. I'm a gardener and it's phenomenal. It's so quiet. It takes me to another place. During the day, I have to deal with personnel, litigation, and other tough stuff. But when I get home I can go out to the garden, take a glass of wine with me, and have a few acres to decompress."

Your sanctuary may look different from this, which is fine. The point, of course, is to find the one that works for you. And often it will be at home.

Our home is the place we know best. It is the place that we have chosen and decorated to fit our needs and tastes. It may be filled with bookshelves and throw pillows, or it may be sleek and laden with technological gadgets. It doesn't matter as long as it's the best place for you to live your blissful life…even when nobody is watching.

BLISS BIT

"I always say I live a blessed life. It means that when I get up in the morning I feel like I have meaning, like I'm impacting and improving the lives of other people. I'm so blessed to have the opportunity to do that."

CHAPTER 16

Tying It All Together

"I love everything I do."

—BLISSFUL MAN IN HIS 20S

WELL, HERE WE ARE.

The end…and the beginning.

Before we part ways for now, let us review in brief where we are. Where things stand. Where you stand.

First…you are an awesome person. Not because you've achieved it, but because you were born as it. You are a human being who is lovely and creative and smart. You are here to live your life. And bliss is what living this life is all about. And, when it comes to that bliss, you now know…

…that finding bliss is not about reaching some unattainable, traditional notion of work/life balance. That, my friend, is bogus. You cannot have *it all*. And you don't want to. What you want is *your all*, to create a life stew that includes your favorite things…your best career and your best set of relationships, your best hobbies and skills. Your best is your bliss. The rest is not. This means that you…

…must make choices. You must decide just what *your all* is, just what will make up your life stew. And you've done that.

You've made your choices and know the changes that will get you on your path to find greater bliss. You know it won't be easy, but you will do it anyway because you know that in the end it will be worth it. Plus you have people around you and tools in your toolkit to help you along the way. And, as you go…

…you will remember that bliss is not a destination, but your lifelong journey. You know that life is not about keeping your eye on the prize, but that life itself *is* the prize. And you're going to live it blissfully every step of the way. This means you will not let your guard down, you will check in with yourself, you will recognize what is working and what is not working for you as you continue on, and you will make intentional, forward movement toward greater bliss. At every turn. And you will do it with grace and a smile.

Thank you for being a part of this process. I am honored to have shared this time with you. I applaud all of the work you've done to get yourself to a blissful place.

And I am excited for you…because I know that real balance, the kind that will make you feel sane, will make you feel peaceful, is yours. I know that bliss, the kind that will give you energy at the start of the day and a sense of satisfaction and happiness at the end of the day, is yours as well. Or will be soon.

I am excited to see what happens next. Because I know whatever it is will be perfect for you.

So go. Your journey awaits.

Enjoy the ride.

EPILOGUE

I JUST WROTE a book on balance and bliss. And I am in the midst of chaos.

No, really, I'm in the midst of chaos. Right now.

We just landed back in the U.S. after six months away. Hubbie and I are moving into a new home. I'm rebuilding my business. I'm getting ready to publish this book. Things are uncertain. There's a lot of TBD.

Things are messy.

But here's what I learned during my time overseas:

That's life.

That's our beautiful, amazing, blissful life stews.

My time away was one of learning—both from ingesting for myself all of those blissful lessons that you've now read and from living in a new place with new perspectives. (For more on my overseas adventures, and the unexpected drama that sometimes came with them, visit *www.bogusbalance.com*.)

I learned that life isn't just a stew, but that it's at its best when it's a messy one, when it's an ever-changing one. Different parts of our stews take up different amounts of time and energy and focus at different times in our lives. Our stews—our personal and professional lives, our relationships and our communities—blend together in all kinds of combinations on any given day. Sometimes our stew comes out a bit too salty and sometimes it comes out a bit too weak and sometimes it comes out perfectly. We don't know what tomorrow's stew will look like for sure. But that's okay. Because we know it will be blissful. Because we've made the choices necessary to make it so.

And we're all in it together. We're all living our messy stews every single day. Every single one of us.

When we live our blissful stews, and—more importantly—when we make the choices to make every piece of them blissful, the amazing thing that happens is that all of that messiness is bliss in itself.

Being blissful isn't about going back to those neat TV dinner trays, it's not about trying to get to some bogus idea of balance that we can't attain. It's about embracing the messiness, the chaos of it all. We make choices, we plan, and then we live, live, live.

Getting to bliss doesn't necessarily mean getting rid of the chaos. Instead, it's knowing that chaos is part of the ride, part of a life that feeds us. And when we can function well within it, when we have the support we need to handle it, when we take care of ourselves throughout it, the messy stew is absolutely awesome.

In the end we all live in our own stews...the ones we choose to create. So create yours well. Create it with great care. Know that we're all on the same messy ride.

It's just a question of how you choose to go about yours.

So go about it with bliss. And love every messy minute of it.

APPENDIX

Your Blissful Follow-Up

WELL, HELLO THERE!

I'm so pleased you've found your way to this *Bliss Builder* section, which is meant to help you continue your journey. It is not meant to be done immediately upon finishing the book, but after you have been on your blissful journey for a while, made some blissful steps, and are ready to take a look at how it's going and what new changes might lead to even more bliss in your life.

I recommend completing this document three to four weeks after you complete the book, then again every few months in your first year. You'll want to continue using it during regular periods of time to check in. Remember that this exercise is also available at *www.bogusbalance.com*.

If you feel you need a more exhaustive blissful reboot, then repeating all of Section II is a great idea.

So here you are, and you're ready to keep your bliss going strong, yes? Excellent!

BLISS BUILDER EXERCISE
Your Blissful Update

For now, let's begin with some familiar *Bliss Builder* questions. Don't look back over your answers from before. Let this hit you fresh. Answer honestly and without judgment.

Think back over the last three months. Consider all parts of your life stew: your career, your family life, your hobbies, your relationships. Have whatever calendar or planning device you use at the ready so you will remember everything that went down.

1. In general, how are you feeling about your blissful stew? What is working? What is not?

2. How does the makeup of your life stew feel to you? Are you spending too much time on one component? Are you trying to do too much? Are you feeling stressed or dissatisfied most of the time? If so, what kinds of changes will help this?

3. Which parts of your career are now filling you with the most enthusiasm and energy?

4. Which ones do you dread?

5. How is your personal/family life going? What is working well?

6. Is there anything about your personal/family life that is taking away from your bliss? How can you address it?

7. How are you enjoying the interests, hobbies, personal relationships and other self-care components of your life stew? Is there enough? Are you feeling relaxed, recharged and re-centered?

8. What about the components related to the question

above aren't working for you? What might you add, remove or change?

9. How is your team of blissful others working for you? Are you getting what you need? Do you want to add another person or two? Who specifically?

10. Is anybody, on your blissful others team or not, decreasing your bliss in some way? Who? Do you want to take some distance from these individuals? How will you do it?

11. How are you feeling about yourself these days? Are you square with you? Do you know that you are worthy no matter what? If not, then how can you get there? What kind of support would be helpful?

12. How have you been dealing with change and that pesky critical inner voice? Is there anything you need from yourself or your blissful others to help you? Are there any other self-help resources that might help you?

13. Are you having fun these days? Doing what? What's working best?

14. If you're not having fun or if you're not feeling good about yourself, then let's get you back on track! What is getting in the way of this? How can you overcome these challenges? What kind of fun or self-care activities would work best for you now?

15. Is there anything else that is impacting your bliss or lack of it at the moment? What would make your blissful journey better? What do you need to do to get there?

Now, keeping in mind your responses above and noting the themes, complete the following:

1. I am committed to continuing my blissful journey, and I will make the following changes in my life stew:

2. When I achieve this, I will feel this way about it:

3. In order to achieve this, I will need to make the following changes in the next six months:

4. Knowing this, I will make these changes by the following deadlines:

    (Add as many lines as you need to make your blueprint meaningful to you.)

    <u>Change</u>   <u>Date</u>

    1.

    2.

    3.

5. The first step I will take, which I will do within the next 24 hours, is:

6. Knowing that bliss is about having my all and making choices, I also know I will have to sacrifice the following in order to achieve this:

7. Though it may be hard, I will go about dealing with these sacrifices in the following ways:

8. This is exciting! I am energized about this part of my journey because I know it will help me continue to be blissful in the following ways:

Congratulations! You're doing what you must do in your life in order to decrease the bogus, increase the bliss, and enjoy your ride. My blissfuls would be proud.
And so am I.

ACKNOWLEDGMENTS

WRITING A BOOK is a humbling thing.

Actually, *living a life* is a humbling thing. That's because you get to be surrounded by amazing people who do amazing things. All the time. You just have to keep your eyes open.

A whole bunch of these amazing people played a part in the writing of this book. I wish I could name them all...but, alas, I know I must stick with the most prominent players on this particular part of my blissful journey.

And so my undying gratitude goes to...

...my blissfuls. I told them I wouldn't put their names in here, and so I won't. But I will say that they gave me more time, energy, wisdom and enthusiasm for this project than I possibly could have hoped for. Getting to know and learn from them has been quite humbling indeed.

...my dear friends Sue Carter Kahl and Rebecca Heyl, who read the book from start to finish simply because I asked them to. It's a blessing to have people in your life who you can trust to read your delicate, beloved words, and then give it to you straight.

...Vasi Huntalas, for pronouncing so definitively, and when I needed to hear it most, that this is the book I was meant to write at this time in my life. I cannot overstate how many times I returned to that moment during this process.

...Bethany Brown of The Cadence Group, for both her incredible marketing assistance and her keen ability to answer every random question with speed and poise.

...my lovely mother, Patricia Costa, for modeling the beauty of bliss from the very beginning.

...my beloved father, Thomas Maloney, who taught me how to live the delicate, blissful balance of grit and grace.

...and Hubbie, who sat with me in multiple cafes while I battled multiple moments of writer's block, insecurity and other mildly torturous writing crises. He's the one who convinced me to keep my voice authentic in this book despite my inclination to act all fancy-schmancy, the one who inspired the addition of the *Bliss Bits*, and the one who told me he'd love me even if the book just stunk. And then promised me it didn't.

ABOUT THE AUTHOR

 DEIRDRE MALONEY IS a bliss builder who helps people find their truth and live a happier, more successful life. She does it through her work as a published author, national speaker and proud president of Momentum LLC.

Deirdre has used her brand of "mild audacity" to inspire positive change and blissful living around the country, presenting keynotes and workshops for organizations including the National Association of Women Business Owners, Vistage International and the Boys and Girls Clubs of America.

Deirdre's other books include *Tough Truths: The 10 Leadership Lessons We Don't Talk About* and *The Mission Myth: Building Nonprofit Momentum Through Better Business*. Her popular blog on all things leadership is a hit with those who likes a direct, authentic style with their morning coffee, and is featured regularly at *www.huffingtonpost.com*.

In her spare time Deirdre can be found running into canyons for greater endurance, meditating in silence for greater peace of mind, exploring new places for greater wisdom, or quietly falling asleep on the couch while her husband shrewdly changes the channel to some kind of silly sci-fi show.

For more information on Deirdre, visit:
www.makemomentum.com